In Search of Mary

The Mother of All Journeys

BEE ROWLATT

ALMA BOOKS

ALMA BOOKS LTD
Hogarth House
32–34 Paradise Road
Richmond
Surrey TW9 1SE
United Kingdom
www.almabooks.com

First published by Alma Books Limited in 2015
© Bee Rowlatt, 2015

Bee Rowlatt asserts her moral right to be identified as the author of this work in accordance with the Copyright, Designs and Patents Act 1988

Printed and bound by CPI Group (UK) Ltd, Croydon, CR0 4YY

ISBN: 978-1-84688-378-1
eBook ISBN : 978-1-84688-385-9

CONTENTS

FOR JUSTIN:

MY OTHER HALF, MY BEST MATE,

MY LOVE

In Search of Mary

The Mother of All Journeys

Advertisement prefacing *Letters Written during a Short Residence in Sweden, Norway, and Denmark*:

The writing travels, or memoirs, has ever been a pleasant employment; for vanity or sensibility always renders it interesting. In writing these desultory letters, I found I could not avoid being continually the first person – "the little hero of each tale". I tried to correct this fault, if it be one, for they were designed for publication; but in proportion as I arranged my thoughts, my letter, I found, became stiff and affected: I, therefore, determined to let my remarks and reflections flow unrestrained, as I perceived I could not give a just description of what I saw but by relating the effect different objects had produced on my mind and feelings whilst the impression was still fresh.

A person has a right, I have sometimes thought, when amused by a witty or interesting egoist, to talk of himself when he can win on our attention by acquiring our affection. Whether I deserve to rank amongst this privileged number, my readers alone can judge – and I give them leave to shut the book, if they do not wish to become better acquainted with me.

My plan was simply to endeavour to give a just view of the present state of the countries I have passed through, as far as I could obtain information during so short a residence; avoiding those details which, without being very useful to travellers who follow the same route, appear very insipid to those who only accompany you in their chair.

– Mary Wollstonecraft, 1796

Me too.

– Bee Rowlatt, 2015

PART ONE

Chapter One

There's Something about Mary

I'm nineteen, and Paul and Nello are arranging my thong. It's white diamante. We're backstage in a corridor – dancers and musicians are rushing by in both directions. They yank it higher up my bum, chatting across me about my body shape and how I got on in rehearsals:

"She can't do round kicks either, not high enough anyway."

"Well yes, too balletic maybe?"

"Exactly – well, it's not fucking *Swan Lake*, is it."

It really isn't *Swan Lake*. Nello is the entertainment boss at the Isla del Lago Theatre, and Paul is the captain of our troupe. Nello has a bright-black bubble perm and wanders around singing in an open towelling robe and patent shoes. Paul has bouffant hair and a face weathered by sarcasm. And he's taken against me and my offending balletic arms. "Are you a *virgin*?" he sneers. I'm being heaved around like a farm animal, on my second day as a showgirl.

I'm scrabbling at the lower slopes of a steep learning curve. After years of dance training, this is my first ever professional gig. It follows a series of bizarre and innocence-murdering auditions. I'd trail down to London from my hometown of York, following little adverts in the back of *The Stage* newspaper. Some jobs were legit, others were not. It took a while to learn to decipher them. At one audition in London's prestigious Pineapple Studios, we were shown a routine and made to repeat it again and again. After each performance a handful of girls were told to leave. An hour later I was still in, and my fear began to be tempered with a growing sense of triumph. But then the auditioner shouted: "OK girls, it's a topless job. So get them out or leave." Most of the girls obediently peeled down their leotards to reveal their breasts. A few of us walked out. I slowly made my way back to Victoria Coach Station in tears, vowing not to tell my mum.

But finally I've landed a proper job, and here I am. It hasn't got off to the best of starts though. On my arrival, after watching the show, I go backstage into the dressing room to meet my new colleagues. I am met by the reflection of around a dozen almost naked women, staring at me in the large mirrors. Mirrors with – great joy – those light bulbs all around. Sequinned showgirl costumes and headdresses are strewn about like a disco-goddess crime scene. The dancers are still in full stage make-up, with the most enormous eyelashes. They look like those scary dolls with swivelling eyeballs that snap open and shut.

"This is Bee," sighs Paul.

"Hi!" I say brightly, and then, to my very own horror: "I'm, er, taking a year out before university."

The entire row of eyelashes snaps back to the mirrors, as every single one of the dancers blanks me. Anguished pause. They, like everyone else, hate students. And I've just dissed their profession as some kind of gap-year jollity. I stand there for quite a long time. Will any of them ever talk to me again?

And I don't even know how to wear a thong properly. Hence these two, wrenching it up between my buttocks and adjusting me around it. The white diamante bra, the wired backpack with streams of huge feather boas bursting out, and the tiara – these are all very good indeed. And the thong, well, I'll get there. But the silver high heels are a problem. I can't dance in them. From the safety of my hometown and the old dance studios where I spent the hours around school, I've fallen into a parallel universe. Somewhere that is not what it looks from the outside. Somewhere glittery, but very very hard.

I may still be a teenager, but I consider myself pretty worldly – and a feminist to boot. I've got good A Levels and an inspirational mother. I enjoyed a quirky childhood of books and no Barbies. I've done all kinds of other jobs, and can clear a pub at last orders quicker than most. I propelled myself into this world to satisfy my desire to be a dancer, a proper real dancer. The dream of so many young girls. My childhood dream of my future self. And *this* is what it's about?

After a week of rehearsals, I'm still hopeless. I cannot dance in those heels. If you've spent years training with your centre of gravity in one place, that's hard to change. I keep toppling back. I hate the silver shoes, and kick them off after every re-hearsal to examine the day's blisters. My first night gets closer, and one of the dancers, a tall blonde called Debbie, takes me to one side. She warns me in the kindest possible way to keep the shoes on at all times: the gossip is that I may well get sacked and flown back home. The silver shoes go straight back on.

The day of my first show comes and I get furious diarrhoea, an unhappy condition for someone in a small white thong. The fear is so paralysing that I can't eat, and pass the hours praying that I will somehow die on my way to the theatre. Then they'd all be sad and say, "You know, she could've done OK at dancing in heels if she'd only survived that tragic lorry crash."

But I don't get squashed on my way to the theatre. I put on unfeasible quantities of make-up with shaking hands and warm up. The music comes up, we're backstage, the lights come up – and out I burst. Huge feathers and all. Complete panic ensues. The intervening years have kindly blurred this moment: my mind doesn't want to go there. But if I force it, I can see myself lurching around like a hallucinating goat, bumping into other dancers. They are screaming at me, maybe instructions, maybe to get out the fucking way. This is one of the worst memories that I own inside my head. From deep within this agony, I catch sight of the other troupe from the flamenco show. They're watching the whole thing from the wings, eyes wide in delighted horror.

Somehow I survive. Nello says he'll give me a second chance if I work on my high kicks and improve by the next night. I hide from Paul, the jaded captain. Debbie, the tall blonde, comes and gives me a hug, saying she was so scared in her first show she'd been made to stand and pretend to be a tree. She turns out to be a saviour, known to all as Aunty Debbie. Aunty Debbie's been in the business since she was fifteen, but is now the oldest of the dancers and is completely ancient. She's at least twenty-four.

Things get better quickly. I learn about "weigh day", how to keep sweat out of your eyelash glue and how to keep tampon strings invisible during the high kicks. I learn to sleep during the day, not to get suntan lines, not to eat or drink before the show and never, not ever, to get in the way of the principal dancer during a quick change. I move victoriously into a little bedsit flat of my very own, with half a kitchen and a balcony where my diamante laundry hangs out to dry. When I finally nail those pirouettes and round kicks in high heels, I'm there.

We spend long hours in the dressing room with those wonderful mirror lights. Conversations generally range around blowjobs and sexually transmitted diseases, diets (the four-day orange fast versus the one day a week eating only toilet tissue), abortions, anorexia and waxing. These nocturnal ramblings paint a new and foreign landscape. I quietly take it in.

Every so often a cockroach sprints out of the showers and across our dressing room, to be met with a barrage of screams and a blast of toxic spray. The cockroaches are peculiarly large and insistent, and come in a variety of shades. Once we even got a translucent albino one. The spray causes prolonged bouts of acrobatic dying, as though the cockroaches' deaths are their own baroque form of revenge, making us scream even more.

Weeks upon weeks of nightly performances, with never a day off, does strange things to your mind. We create mischief to counter the repetitive strain. One night we experiment with hairpieces, and in the first pirouette my face gets tangled up inside a long blonde ponytail. Another time we "borrow" someone's medication: a dancer has been prescribed local anaesthetic for her toothache, and for fun we all have a go. On stage our lips are so numb we can't close our mouths properly, and every turn releases a flying trail of spit. We choke on snorts of dribbly laughter.

Night after night we sit around sewing our tights, semi-naked in the dressing room, and bare our souls. Bad boyfriends, tricky childhoods, same-sex encounters, boob jobs gone wrong – we discuss it all. These are tough and independent women: none of them are stupid. Yet I am stunned by what they deem acceptable in life – have I been so sheltered until now? There is a general tolerance of starvation in various forms. Abuse is the norm. One dancer's former captain threatened her: "Move your cunt or I'll set fire to your tampon string"; another had ice cubes forced up her vagina by jealous colleagues. She relates this while picking her herpes scabs. These are examined and dreamily flicked away.

One night, the word "feminist" is uttered. Not by me, but I prick up my ears. "No way would I grow hairy legs, bloody lezzers!" is the blistering riposte. Do I leap to feminism's defence? No, I keep quiet, probably gluing on some giant eyelashes. But that doesn't stop me from thinking about it to this day, sometimes adding an alternative ending where I proclaim the sisterhood and convert them all, maybe getting carried aloft on their shoulders.

Something in this flippant remark begins to germinate, deep within. Here I am, in a room full of hungry women on low wages, who've endured public weighings, been called bitches and "fat cows on ice" in front of their colleagues, whose very living depends on being looked at – and if they look down on feminism, what has feminism done wrong? If you can't mention it here, what's the point?

Being a showgirl equipped me with a nascent sense of feminist outrage, and the twin habits of wearing only underwear on a night out and never having to buy a drink. Untroubled by any inherent contradictions, my next stop is Glasgow.

The diva-ish corners are soon knocked off in my new life as a student. I actually have to buy drinks. But I'm still haunted by the dancers' acceptance of physical abuse and casual sexist bullying. Why do they put up with it?

Still wondering this, I have the luck to encounter someone who changes my life. An unforgettable woman of courage, a woman who inspired me then and still does now. A woman who had all the mud thrown in her face but achieved greatness, who was smashed and reviled but kept going, who invented her own life and was, in her words, "the first of a new genus".

Annoyingly she's been dead for a couple of centuries, but that doesn't hold our relationship back. This is where the book comes in. Lights go on when I read it. Entering her world for the first time many years ago set off a chain reaction that's still taking place now. The book was first published in 1796 as *Letters Written during a Short Residence in Sweden, Norway, and Denmark*. This was affectionately abbreviated by the author's future husband to *Letters from Norway*. And as a rollercoaster ride into the life and work of the world's first feminist, it has no equal.

This is the story of how *Letters from Norway* got into my life and took over. This book seeks to proclaim that book, the woman's life and her legacy, and how they came to infiltrate my waking hours. I want you to love her as much as I do. If I could reach out and squeeze your arm I would do it right now. Mary Wollstonecraft does not disappoint. My first reading of *Letters from Norway* is followed by three escalating phases of interest in its author. They are: the Romantics, the Vindication and Motherhood. Handily these are also passing decades, successive life stages. How was I to know that she would be the star and chief informant of all three?

1. Wollstonecraft and the Romantics

Bliss it was in that dawn to be alive, / But to be young was very heaven. I was young when I first read *Letters from Norway*. It influenced the great poets that I was now studying. Romantic literature suits this early life phase, with its intensity and urgent possibilities. The teenage anthem of "it's not fair" is in fact an understatement. This is nothing less than the battle of trying to become yourself. For some of us this doesn't happen again so awkwardly until the day we abruptly turn into parents. Romantic literature, with its quests, iconoclastic visionaries and brave horizons – this is where you need to be for life's big dramas.

It's easy to check whether you yourself are a Romantic (NB: this does not mean people who send Valentine's cards). Look into the sky on a clear night. Some people pick out the constellations they recognize and point them out.

"Look, there's Saturn."

"Are you sure?"

"Yes I am – look, you can tell because X Y Z."

"Oh."

Other people look out for satellites and discernible aeroplane routes. Avoid these people. Some respond with excitement: the outer edges of human understanding are delineated right here. They'll mention a Brian Cox thing they read. These are sexy and confident *New Scientist* types who love a challenge.

But some people look up into a sky full of stars and think: "Oh God, it's just too much – how can any of this be possible?" Their mind reels with all the people who've died beneath these stars and those who are yet to live. Humanity is so vulnerable, so flawed. Nature is so ineffable. Infinity is so... infinite. They might mention the Sublime and other words elevated by capital letters. They feel a spiky restlessness, deep inside a mystery internal organ. This person is a Romantic.

I was in the right place to identify this. In the furthest-away university, with the darkest weather and most glowering Gothic spires. The elements drive right into your face. It's a fact that Glaswegian rain falls in all directions at once, even upwards. The baffling depth of the winters, the soaring stone tenements blackened by the years and the savage landscapes beyond – this was the place for *sensibility*. This was right up my moody street.

The undergrad literature curriculum at Glasgow University had something for everyone, even people who like aeroplane routes. Among its many genres are the Romantic, the Medieval and the Augustan. Over a plastic pint in the corner of the Queen Margaret Union bar we'd imagine these three categories as blokes. First comes a dark hero, a-roving on a galloping horse. He's a lover and a fighter, and he never gets old. Behind him comes a monk croaking in Latin, telling bawdy fart jokes on the side. He, in turn, is pursued by a desiccated old grammarian in a wig, who mocks everything in sight.

So it's pretty obvious which one you're going to fall for. And I fell hard. I heard about some upstart woman called Mary Wollstonecraft, who wrote a kind of travel book made out of letters. Its portrayals of the Sublime, of wild and terrifying nature, drew rave reviews. It was a bestseller, and the young Romantics couldn't get enough. The poet Robert Southey breathlessly asked a friend: "Have you met with Mary Wollstonecraft's *Letters from Sweden and Norway*? She has made me in love with a cold climate, and frost and snow, with a northern moonlight." Coleridge channelled her straight into his *Kubla Khan*. William Godwin wrote: "If ever there was a book calculated to make a man in love with its author, this appears to me to be the book."

My first reading of *Letters from Norway* proved unforgettable. Like Godwin I promptly fell in love, but for different reasons. Right there in the introduction, where naturally I was seeking shortcuts, was the real motive behind this apparently jaunty trip of hers. In the worn edition I still use today, the evidence of my youthful astonishment remains. The following words are underlined in stupid green ink: "In fact, Wollstonecraft was on a treasure hunt in Scandinavia." *A treasure hunt*. That single phrase hooked me. A treasure hunt. Has there been another treasure-hunting single-mum philosopher on the high seas?

But the Romantics don't just caper around gasping at mountains and starry skies. They also go out and try to change the world. Which brings us to:

2. Wollstonecraft and the *Vindication*

The next time Wollstonecraft electrifies my life it's via *A Vindication of the Rights of Woman*. This is her best-known work, and feminism's first manifesto. It was published in 1792 and soon quoted around the world, even by the American president. And it's blisteringly angry. Reading it again among the doldrums of my early career felt like being in the same room as an intoxicating but terrifying woman. A taster description of fluttering girly types:

> *Fragile in every sense of the word, they are obliged to look up to man for every comfort. In the most trifling danger they cling to their support, with parasitical tenacity, piteously demanding succour; and their natural protector extends his arms, or lifts up his voice, to guard the lovely trembler – from what? Perhaps the frown of an old cow, or the jump of a mouse.*

Stand back – you'll get scorn in your eyes. Some of it's funny, some of it is weird, the rest is very powerful. Admittedly she spends time on topics unlikely to vex today's youngsters, such as "Does woman have a soul?" and "Does God want women to be inferior?" But elsewhere she could not be fresher. When she demands "JUSTICE for one half of the human race", Wollstonecraft is talking about equal rights to education and financial independence.

In the middle of one of her scraps with Jean-Jacques Rousseau (who argues it's their lovely quiet pretty softness that gives the ladies power over men), she delivers the killer blow that's still feminism's bottom line to this day:

> *I do not wish [women] to have power over men, but over themselves.*

Power… over themselves. Are we there yet? This question of power over ourselves still needs a proper stare in the face. The

Vindication is a tonic for anyone who's twenty-something and a bit vague: if there were a curriculum for such people, she'd be top of the list. The final distillation is: woman up. Get educated. Be useful. And, above all, independence is "the grand blessing of life".

For me, the book was a kick in the backside at the right moment. In the thick of trying to achieve "power over myself", after the year as a showgirl my next professional gig, inexplicably, is journalism. From a job where you get looked at, to a job where you get shouted at. It's my mid-twenties, and I'm paying the rent by making live news programmes for the BBC World Service.

The wages are lower than showgirl wages, and the management equally incomprehensible. Our boss emerges, tells us how much he misses journalism, then goes back into his office to do more managing. We roll our eyes and get back to work. His sole piece of career advice is to elaborate on job applications precisely how I will make his life easier.

On the upside, the colleagues are exceptional. The World Service in the 1990s is the most exciting place. It still lives in Bush House – home to exiles, poets, eccentrics and rebels from all over the world. As a rookie in the Latin American Service, I'm taught to razor-cut audiotape by a bass-voiced Chilean and a Mexican Goth. The African Services have legendary parties. The Russians never answer the phone. The Arabs smoke more than any smokers have ever smoked, anywhere. The head of the Uzbek Service wears a famous hat and translates Shakespeare. There are marble staircases and stained threadbare carpets. No high-camp sequinned glamour, but also no undignified thong adjustments. Swings and roundabouts, I reflect sagely.

There are female bosses, and there are female correspond-ents. But very few. Reporting is still largely a posh bloke's game, and the women who do make it aren't necessarily of the sisterly kind. One producer, on hearing the flat-vowelled beauty of what remains of my Yorkshire accent, shouts "Give 'er a bag o' greasy chips!" And there's an unforgettable female presenter who goes out of her way to crush the ideas, hopes and even the most timid utterances of her junior female col-leagues. This includes me, and I spend much of the two years I work on her programme wanting to throw up.

One day this presenter holds up the interview brief I've written between her finger and thumb, waves it at our editor and acidly pronounces:

"I've done what you *might* call some *basic journalism* on this *story*, and it turns out that *Law in Action* did it *two weeks* ago."

I quietly call *Law in Action* and find out that this is not true. But it's too late. The editor won't stick up for an idea that the presenter has so thoroughly murdered. There's nothing to do but take the humiliation and grind my teeth.

If you are feeling downtrodden, try a prescription-free dip into the pages of the *Vindication*. It's a resolve-firming, terri-fying boost. Like sticking your head out of a car window into a hailstorm of indignation. It may sting, but your complaints will pale next to what she had to put up with. Sometimes she can't contain herself, and adds an asterisk so she can blow off more steam at the bottom of the page (*what nonsense!* etc.) You will feel better for it.

Wollstonecraft herself has to stick with jobs she hates, and is no stranger to people pulling rank on her. As a governess to the richest family in Ireland, the Kingsboroughs, she attends one of their social gatherings. A guest engages with her, this lively, dark-eyed young woman with a dazzling mind and a knowing sense of humour. The aristocrat only finds out later, face turning ashen, that she was accidentally conversing with the *staff*. Wollstonecraft's parting shot to these people is an unflattering cameo in her next book, as she goes on to become a celebrated author. Ha!

This is how Wollstonecraft is still so compelling: she defies categories, she constantly bounces back and reinvents herself. She keeps finding out new treasure to hunt. She's always pushing the boundaries of gender and class. What she's doing is what we now call human rights and social mobility. What drives Wollstonecraft onwards? In spite of all the raging, it is love. Love: her "ardent affection for the human race" and her passion for its improvement.

Wollstonecraft remains quite poor throughout her life, but still manages to set up a school, travel alone, publish reviews and books, and live in Paris during the Revolution. She keeps on going. On top of supporting her family, and regular career breaks caring for whoever was about to die or have a baby (or both, in the case of her first love and best friend Fanny). She just keeps on going. This entirely rocks my twenty-something world.

3. Wollstonecraft and Motherhood

The third and decisive phase of my Wollstonecraft love-in centres on what Virginia Woolf calls her "experiments in living". Her unusual domestic arrangements include attempting a *ménage à trois*, her love for other women, having a baby out of wedlock, and even having the effrontery to call unannounced at the house of a man she rather liked, without a chaperone. These days our twenties are a series of misadventures in co-existence. Isn't that what being young is for? Back then, such things get her into lots of trouble.

Of all Wollstonecraft's life experiments, the one into motherhood is most moving. This is the one that sets me spiralling off on my mission. Some time in my thirties I read Virginia Woolf's essay about Wollstonecraft, and the fascination floods back. "Mary's life had been an experiment from the start, an attempt to make human conventions conform more closely to human needs." Approaching the age at which Wollstonecraft died, I reckon I finally know what this means, this "experiments in living": it's discovering how best to share your life with other people.

Including small people. Motherhood happens to me at twenty-nine; four kids later I'm still catching up. It happens, as for many women, just as I am getting "power over myself". Everything changes. My pre-dancer self, who enjoyed certainty and knew all injustices could be solved – where has she gone? Yes, it's your basic mum-life crisis. The 1970s having-it-all heritage suddenly doesn't fit. I begin to doubt feminism, and suffer from laundry-related rages. I feel unrepresented, guilty for letting the side down, and annoyed about feeling guilty.

I'm drawn back to *Letters from Norway* and the journey that Wollstonecraft makes, both on and behind its pages. I daydream about her Scandinavian treasure hunt, with her baby. The letters from the rocky and remote shores detailing people, food, nature and politics. Her moments of madness and high passion, interspersed with dry social statistics. All this with a baby in tow. The woman pulled off multitasking before the notion was invented. I return again to those heart-felt, funny and demanding letters, but this time I'm not on a Sublime thrill-seeker's mission. This time I only want to know one thing: how the hell did she do it?

Having a baby doesn't stop Wollstonecraft writing or cramp her style in the least. Of course she does it the modern way, packing in an extra decade of travel and work-related madness before getting knocked up. She's thirty-four, living in violent revolutionary France and dating the baby's father, a dodgy two-timing American. Career versus motherhood? What*ever*. She simply scoops the baby up and takes it along on her Scan-dinavian adventure. She breast-feeds, which wasn't fashionable at the time, and between writing books and trying to change the world she thinks a lot about children.

Despite her own appalling childhood (domestic violence and hours spent sitting in silent fear), Wollstonecraft becomes a tender and enthusiastic parent. She doesn't limit the care to her own, either. She wants to change the way everyone brings up children, to create future "rational beings". The first book that she writes is, after all, *Thoughts on the Education of Daughters*.

Here am I, stuck in a self-regarding web of conflicting im-pulses, pitting motherhood against selfhood. And Wollstone-craft has it nailed long before mothers like me began carping about their diminishing horizons. I begin to think about her, and find her invading my rare private moments. Aghast, I read about her death. It's the most bitter blow. A few years after her first baby, she gets pregnant again and dies, cruelly, unnecessarily, in childbirth. She's only thirty-eight. Mary Wollstonecraft campaigns, writes and dies for motherhood. She achieves remarkable motherhood – and then it kills her. She's the mother of all mothers.

The baby who goes to Scandinavia with her in *Letters from Norway* is not much older than my youngest child, Will. Suddenly, ping! The revelation lands. This is what to do. This is how to move beyond the thinking, and the talking avidly in pubs about Wollstonecraft, to actually doing something. Here's the way to illustrate her. She took her baby on that notorious Scandinavian voyage? OK, then I'll do it too. I will recreate that trip. Just like her, with my own baby and everything.

Chapter Two

Half a Million Small Things

After a short silence that took a long time coming, I casually tell my husband Justin about the plan. Just this small plan – that I've been, you know, planning. The plan is that I want to go off with baby Will and retrace the eighteenth-century Scandinavian adventures of Mary Wollstonecraft. And her baby. He laughs:

"It's brilliant."

I frown. "But won't you miss me – I mean, how will everyone cope without me? It'll be at least ten days, maybe even longer: what about all the laundry and packed lunches and homework and other stuff, you know – there's some school trips coming up, and also Eva's dance exam, and of course the girls will miss me so much. So you'll probably need me here, won't you. Won't you?"

"No. We'll be fine. Go for it."

Damn. Now we've got to do it. Before I attempt to raise the notion with the kids, it brings itself up. A morning, like any other – shouting, spilling breakfast, shoes and book bags in a heap. The eight-year-old asks:

"Where's daddy?"

"He's away working."

"Again?"

"Yes."

"He's always away!"

"Well, that's not true. But his journalism does involve rather a lot of fabulous and exotic travel, now you mention it."

"Yeah, and your job is always in the same place, isn't it – ha-ha, mummy gets to go on the Northern Line. Why don't mums travel as much as dads?"

"They do, of course – they do! Just I – *eat your breakfast*."

Deep breath once all three girls are safely in school and I'm pushing the baby back home. And I start to wonder: who are the travelling mums? Even the richest ones I know don't do it: just take off travelling. They do loads of other stuff, but not that. Don't they want to? Is it all down to money? Is it that we can't? Or we just don't?

I head to the bookshelf. There she is. The very sight of the spine of the book reassures me. The book is now in my hands. *Letters from Norway*. It flops open at favourite points and mementoes fall out, faded scraps of previous readings. A postcard. A receipt. For a moment the world readjusts around me as I skim the pages, back and forth. I find a sense of balance. And a vague feeling of indebtedness. This book is our portal. I look at Will:

"They did it – and we can do it." I wave the book at him. "This is our treasure hunt." Will snores gently.

I don't have an excuse not to go. And the more I think about it, the better it gets. We'll follow Wollstonecraft, retracing her steps, spying into her personal life and celebrating her public achievements, as possibly the best woman who ever lived. I have an urge to tell the world about her adventures, and these passionate experiments in living. I am hoping to soak up some of her thoughts, to realize her, to get close to her. I'm basically a groupie.

But there's a problem. How will I get any actual words written with a baby in tow? Will is nearly ten months old and a vigorous crawler. What if he falls into a pond while I'm contemplating the Sublime? Or eats a discarded cigarette as I'm marking a sacred footstep where Wollstonecraft trod? This is the reality of motherhood. If I never get this thing done, it will be because Will had a bad night, or wouldn't eat and then got food all over both of us, or because he was struggling with a red face and a full nappy, and only I could make his life good (the best power of them all).

This is the thing. Countless days of women's lives vanish into the haze of a new baby, exhausted toddler or anxious child. Sometimes there's simply nothing left, no time left over, no separate sense of self. If I wasn't so knackered, this would really get my dander up. It's how mothers live: in the gaps between other people's lives. Our essence is absorbed into theirs. But despite my grumbling, one thing is clear: an absorbed life is very much worth living. Indeed, this makes it better than it was. Somehow we're not diminished: life is brighter, louder and altogether better.

But what about that tiredness, the amazing and famous tiredness of parenthood, so boring for everyone else and yet so fundamentally defining when it's happening to you? Has anyone ever been this tired? Is it possible to die of tiredness? Lack of sleep and constant vigilance over a baby starting to crawl can combine to vanquish pretty much anything an adult human might attempt. He's so small, but the magnetic force of him radiates hugely in my life. I think about the dimples in his arms and sense the win-win: if I never get this thing done, I will still have him.

The trip is now happening. I've told everyone and spent many stolen hours setting it up, so it must. Luckily my day job at the World Service is freelance these days, and therefore flexible. Families, however, don't share this quality, and I have to keep finding new hiding places to get stuff done. We're due to set off in two weeks. My lists of instructions, advice, emergency numbers and school contacts are getting borderline freaky. Both Justin and Nori, our part-time nanny, repeatedly assure me that everyone will somehow cope.

While I cavort with baby Will, who is masquerading as Wollstonecraft's baby Frances, we leave behind Will's three sisters, Eva, Zola and Elsa, and their increasingly complicated social lives. The travel plans are squeezed around them: we'll be leaving after Elsa's assembly, and getting back just before Eva's birthday. I point this out loudly and often, to make myself seem less selfish. No one is remotely bothered.

We hit an early logistics problem. In the interests of authenticity we must approach Norway from the sea, as Wollstonecraft did. But there are no longer any ferries to Norway from the UK. So Will and I must fly into neighbouring Sweden, then catch a ferry that's 165 kilometres away. Between the plane landing and the ferry setting sail we have roughly six hours. But there's no direct connection, and the combination of buses and trains adds up to over five hours.

I'm conveying this in relentless detail to a friend. She looks at me, then says she wouldn't really be interested in reading a book about a woman with a baby missing a bus. "It's not exactly *Touching the Void*, is it Bee?" No, maybe not. But for the record, the *Touching the Void* bloke may have broken most of his bones, but did he do it carrying a ten-month-old baby who smells of poo – poo that may well have squeezed out into several layers of clothing? No, he did not. So give it a rest with the "me and my broken bones", thank you.

What is it with mountains anyway? I've always been a bit taken aback by the part in the *Vindication* where Wollstonecraft concedes that the greatest public works have proceeded from unmarried and childless men and women. But, she adds:

> *The welfare of society is not built upon extra-ordinary exertions; and were it more reasonably organized, there would be still less need of great abilities, or heroic virtues.*

Which I choose to read as follows: instead of conquering something very very big, how about: get the kettle on, then conquer half a million small things. Like most of us do, most days.

Why isn't Mary Wollstonecraft as famous as she ought to be? She has a habit of attracting eccentrics and boffins, historians and feminist theorists. Tantalizing company no doubt, but she deserves a much wider fan base. Look how everyone adores her near-contemporary, Jane Austen. They're choosing the view into a tidy garden over one onto a crashing sea. Have courage, readers! That Woolf again: "If Jane Austen had lain as a child on the landing to prevent her father from thrashing her mother [as Wollstonecraft did], her soul might have burned with such a passion against tyranny that all her novels might have been consumed in one cry for justice."

And then there's her daughter, who wrote one of the most enduring novels of all time. Yes, a lot of people don't know that Mary Wollstonecraft, on top of everything else, is *Frankenstein*'s granny. Yet despite everything she has remained in the cobwebby shadows, rarely visible – and regularly misspelt. The biographies of her are magnificent, but they're mainly for people who read magnificent biographies. How to rescue her from the dust? Would a few mirror lights and a glitter-ball help get the *Vindication* out there?

My very first Mariac encounter gives me inspiration and doubt in equal measure. It's an event at the Stoke Newington Literary Festival. The festival is a celebration of the radical London neighbourhood where Wollstonecraft lived and worked, and where happily she now gets her own gig.

I arrive early, all a-flutter, as the first contributor is preparing for her reading. She has a shawl draped loosely over her shoulders, presumably to channel Mary Wollstonecraft. I look around. The woman on the door also has a shawl, and so does the woman giving out teabags with poetic phrases attached. I inwardly kick myself: why don't I have a Wollstonecraft shawl? They're obviously throwing some kind of gang sign.

The first reader gives a galloping account of Wollstonecraft's life, then there's a statue campaign. Then two installation artists talk about their projects, and finally we're all urged to chat to one another. It's all a bit earnest, and sparsely attended. I'm torn. On one hand I unreservedly admire the contributors for trying to bring her to new audiences. But on the other, Wollstonecraft deserves so more than this. She deserves a more convincing, a more resounding, a more fabulous, great, big, clanging, sky-rocketing, flame-throwing, heart-bursting memorial. Not a handful of ladies in a warm wooden room.

Taking advantage of the allotted chat time I approach the person who spoke about Wollstonecraft's life, and congratulate her. The woman is Roberta Wedge, the Wollstonecraft blogger, and it turns out that she's something rather special. Emboldened by our joint adventures in adoration, I casually ask if she'd like to have a coffee some time. She says yes, and I leave with a spring in my step. I'm going on a Wollstonecraft date!

Roberta chooses the place of our meeting: the café inside the towering Gothic splendour of St Pancras station. I rush in with my high-vis bike gear flapping, and she's already sitting there in a composed, somehow old-fashioned way. It all feels a bit special interest. Roberta's face is old and young all at once: sweet, with dimples, radiating quaintness – and somehow out of kilter with the world, at least the bustling King's Cross world outside.

"Wollstonecraft's grave is just a few minutes away from here," says Roberta, and as our coffees arrive, we launch off. The first thing we put to rights is that Wollstonecraft's memory has been failed, and that a reboot is most definitely in order.

"What the world needs is *Wollstonecraft: The Movie*," says Roberta. "What elements of a Hollywood blockbuster does her life not contain? Sex? No problem. Violence? We've got the

French Reign of Terror. What could be more violent? The only thing it doesn't have is a fast car chase, but I'm sure we could arrange something with the time her stage coach overturns..."

Roberta used to work in higher education. "Mary has given me a new project, a new life." I get the sense she almost lives *as* her, or at least through her. She speaks in elegant paragraphs as academics do, but with a "right?" at the end of her sentences, which lessens the feeling of a lecture. It draws me in and makes me feel that we're in cahoots. I ask what most inspires her about Wollstonecraft.

"She made her way as a young woman without resources, moving around a lot, living in other people's spaces, as a governess, as a lady's companion, and always struggling and striving to the betterment not just of herself but of others around her." We nod in vigorous agreement. "She knew injustice from her earliest days," Roberta goes on. "She knew that what her father was doing to her mother was not right, but she didn't have a framework to put that into. Until she moved to Newington Green, in what is now London. She became part of this village of high-minded anti-establishment Dissenters, who wanted to create a better society. So what's not to love?"

Roberta also tweets in the actual person of Wollstonecraft, listening out for people who mention her and replying in her voice. Generally they are students having to write an essay, and often they can't spell her name. But nonetheless up pops Roberta in full eighteenth-century mode, asking how she can help. Sometimes she is sought out directly. I ask how she knows what to say.

"I try to project, based on the texts. For example I was approached on Twitter about the SlutWalk. In reply I gave them soundbites of Wollstonecraft's opinions on modesty." She pauses. "I never heard back."

Wollstonecraft's not all about disapproval, though. She's often mischievous, and she enjoys the beauty of people she meets on her travels. Especially noteworthy is her observation that women in their thirties are hotter – the "perfect state" of "majestic seriousness" – than their twenty-something counterparts. By my calculations, if we allow for inflation, then these days that sexy majestic seriousness lasts well beyond our forties. Result.

Roberta lives alone and far from her family. After losing her job, she started her Wollstonecraft blog on the anniversary of Wollstonecraft's death. "I'm not obsessed..." she says lightly, and not for the last time. I don't mind if she is or not. I've been Wollstonecrafting in solitude for so long that I get carried away, overexcited with the companionship of the moment.

"Do you actually want to make her be alive – to bring her back?"

Roberta hesitates, but doesn't pick up on my half-baked hopes of a séance. "I think the world would be better if there were more people in it like her, willing to stand up and speak out, willing to take a risk."

I feel foolish, as though I'd tried to invoke Wollstonecraft's ghostly presence with us right here at the table with our flat white coffees and lemon cakes. Nonetheless I leave this encounter completely abuzz. She's among us – she's alive on social media: Wollstonecraft is at large. I've found a comrade, indeed a fan club, after all the lonesome admiring.

I hop on my bike, rushing back for my childcare deadline, and cycle past the back of St Pancras Old Church. After a dark railway tunnel, near an ugly house with white vans outside, is a row of steps and a heavy iron gate. On the other side of the gate – it's right there. It's necessary to stop here, and have a moment for Wollstonecraft's gravestone. Like her, it may be old and modest, but it's real, and it's here. Her remains have since been reburied in Bournemouth, but I greet her anyway, waving merrily as though she can see me...

Chapter Three:

"I Feel Myself Unequal to the Task"

I'm leaving on the trip next week. I'm starting to need a deep breath when I say it. The trip. Next week. Just remind myself again – what, exactly, am I letting myself in for? Flip open my well-thumbed copy of *Letters from Norway*.

It's June 1795. Europe is at war. Wollstonecraft sets off, with only her baby, Frances, and her maid, Marguerite, for company. They're travelling from Hull to Sweden, and onwards to Norway, in an increasingly precarious combination of wobbly boats and strangers' carriages. Along the way she writes the series of letters that will become her bestselling book. It's a journey that most men would balk at: highwaymen and pirates are still very much at large. But not Wollstonecraft:

I enter a boat with the same indifference as I change horses, and as for danger, come when it may, I dread it not suffi- ciently to have any anticipating fears.

She's putting on a brave face, though. Scared of boats, horses or pirates? No, she fears something far worse. Her deepest fear is losing her love, and her whole faith in love. Wollstonecraft has a shattered heart.

Here's the story behind *Letters from Norway*. That dodgy American boyfriend of hers? Gilbert Imlay. He's a tall, handsome frontiersman who claims he was a captain in the American War of Independence. Gilbert. A proper cad's name. They get together in Paris, where Wollstonecraft has moved to be at the heart of the Revolution. And although she questions the institution, they pretend to be married. This way his Rev-friendly nationality can shelter her, as Paris becomes increasingly violent.

While Wollstonecraft has been hanging with radical luminaries, writing, learning French, avoiding the Terror and getting knocked up by Imlay, he's been doing business. Nice little earner. Paris is starving, and he's smuggling silverware – fresh from head-chopped aristos – out of France and through the blockade to neutral Scandinavia to be exchanged for corn. He leaves Wollstonecraft and their new baby behind for months on end, through one of the coldest winters on record. The Seine freezes over. Wollstonecraft and her baby are cold and poor, and foreign.

Imlay has a lot on his mind, you see. One of his ships has gone missing. A ship laden with silver. Back and forth he goes, between Paris, Le Havre and London, and the letters that follow him get more and more shrill. Wollstonecraft just isn't so much fun now she's got all these expectations of him. Imlay's business and personal lives may be demanding, but he still finds time to shack up with an actress. Wollstonecraft finds out and despairs, and tries to kill herself with laudanum.

Imlay spots a way to get her out of his hair and score himself a freebie at the same time. You've got to admire him: "Come

on love, get yourself out of town for a while – you can do me
a little errand while you're at it! Just a missing ship off the
coast of Norway. Sea air's what you need. And find my ship
for me, there's a good girl." Kisses her pale forehead. Suddenly
thinks of a sweetener: "I know, why don't I come and join
you afterwards? We could have a little holiday together – how
about Switzerland?" He saunters out the door whistling a
revolutionary ditty. Oh, she wants him back. She starts packing for the voyage.

This, then, is the story behind the glorious treasure trail.
And it stirs a mix of strange and bad feelings in me. Her book
never mentions the treasure. *Letters from Norway* is arranged
as a series of letters to a "dear friend". She doesn't name him,
but they are obviously addressed to Imlay. In Letter One, Wollstonecraft, baby Frances and Marguerite the maid are already
in trouble. After eleven days aboard a boat not intended for
passenger travel, bad weather means they can't continue to
Norway as planned. The captain wants instead to carry onwards to Denmark. But Wollstonecraft has other ideas. She
wants them to row her to shore right here:

> *I exerted all my rhetoric to prevail on the captain to let me
> have the ship's boat, and though I added the most forcible
> of arguments, I for a long time addressed him in vain.*

You just know this is true. She harangues him, deploying one
tactic after another, while he grimly stares at the horizon. He
is thinking: I should never have let them on board. If I ignore
her for long enough, surely she will stop talking. But she does

not stop, despite her dark hair whipping into her eyes and mouth. Finally, he rolls his eyes upwards. He is, after all, a good-natured man, according to Wollstonecraft. He gestures for her to talk to his crew. The ship's sailors do her bidding "with all alacrity", she triumphantly notes, overlooking the possibility that they can't wait to get rid of her. They row her, the baby and the maid to land.

This was not the plan. They're now in the Swedish middle of nowhere. Looking out for any "vestige of a human habitation", Marguerite timidly points out that there is none to be seen. Wollstonecraft snaps – "I did not listen to her" – and marches onto the rocky wild shore. This is how it happens in the book. In a private letter to Imlay, however, she describes how, shortly after landing, she is exhausted and falls down in a faint, injuring her head on a rock. But she's not down for long.

By Letter Two, Wollstonecraft has already made her way from that rocky landing to a Lieutenant's cottage, befriended his wife, slept in a juniper-strewn room and drunk illegal coffee. They are now in Gothenburg. Despite the frequent sadness of the book, parts of it are very funny. She's often extravagantly rude. She is particularly preoccupied with Scandinavian teeth, regularly reporting their badness:

The quantity of coffee, spices and other things of that kind, with want of care, almost universally spoil their teeth, which contrast but ill with their ruby lips.

In Gothenburg she has to sit and eat for several hours, as "dish after dish is changed, in endless rotation, and handed round with solemn pace to each guest". Eventually, fed to exhaustion, she begs her hosts to let her escape for a walk. "Well!" they surely tut, when she leaves the room. "Did you see how she poked at the meat? She asks *man's* questions. No wonder she's single." (Wollstonecraft's barbs on "very fat" Swedish women are still causing outrage five years later, according to the French wag de La Tocnaye in his own Scandi travel book.)

Later, along with some thoughtful gardening tips and a rousing attack on the way Swedish people treat their servants, Wollstonecraft turns in some observations on Swedish gender politics: "The men stand up for the dignity of man," she remarks, "by oppressing the women." Swedish women have lives of abject drudgery, their hands crack and bleed from washing clothes in icy river water. And will the menfolk help them? Not a chance: it would "disgrace their manhood."

As she travels north to Strömstad, she is regularly and powerfully assaulted by the "detestable evaporations" of the local farmland fertilizer. It's made out of "putrefying herrings", and is so stinky that even when dining indoors – perhaps developing a profound line of thought on the perfectibility of mankind – the smell gets in, distracting and irritating her.

And then there's the duvet. The first ever time I read *Letters from Norway* I nearly shouted with laughter when I realized what she was talking about:

The beds ... were particularly disagreeable to me. It seemed to me that I was sinking into a grave when I entered them; for, immersed in down placed in a sort of box, I expected to be suffocated before morning.

Mary Wollstonecraft was quite possibly the first British woman ever to sleep under a duvet. But there's much more than mad bedding and smelly fish. There's the Sublime, the wild beauty of Wollstonecraft's landscapes. She's travelling in June, marvelling at "the beauty of the northern summer's evening and night". There are frequent crunching gear changes, like this one, from irritation straight into contemplative awe:

Arrived at the ferry, we were still detained; for the people who attend at the ferries have a stupid kind of sluggishness in their manner, which is very provoking when you are in haste. At present I did not feel it; for scrambling up the cliffs, my eye followed the river as it rolled between the grand rocky banks; and to complete the scenery, they were covered with firs and pines, through which the wind rustled, as if it were lulling itself to sleep with the declining sun.

She especially loves the pines.

I feel myself unequal to the task of conveying the beauty and elegance of the scene where the spiral tops of the pines are loaded with ripening seed and the sun gives a glow to their light-green tinge, which is changing into purple, one tree more or less advanced, contrasting with another...

Reading this, I also feel myself unequal, in ways I struggle to explain. How, for example, can she be suicidal, yet also the most optimistic person I've ever met? She radiates such purpose in her writings and actions. Usefulness is a favourite word. A key part of her philosophy is the principle of human perfectibility. And, gently mocking herself, her "favourite subject of contemplation" is nothing less than "the future improvement of the world". Truly the woman is no slouch. I feel myself thinking and existing in slow motion, a snail meandering after a comet-like blaze. Where does she find the will to carry on? How can you be a suicidal optimist?

A smaller, quieter doubt nags at my mind as I read. What sort of company will she be? She's pretty bloody scary at times. Can I do justice to her emotional burdens and plumb the depths of those extravagant mood swings? There's the journey – and then there's The Journey. The Hollywood-Voiceover Journey. Where you have to get crushed and cry and then become a better person. The quiet doubt suggests that I'm unlikely to have sufficient capacity to keep up with her. "You're too shallow," it whispers. And I am. So I listen for a moment then think about something else.

Like the practical side: a few tantalizing hints are sprinkled in about her immediate purpose. There are references here and there to her "business". What exactly is going on? Here's what we now know: Imlay has licensed a French ship with Norwegian papers and a Norwegian crew. It sets sail with a cargo of aristocratic silver from revolutionary France to neutral Sweden, where they can trade it for corn.

But the ship goes missing, last heard of in the care of the Norwegian captain, Peder Ellefsen. Ellefsen has since reappeared and is swanning around Norway saying he knows nothing about it. Imlay wants his silver and his ship. He gives Wollstonecraft the legal authority to represent him, and to collect money or damages on his behalf. Wollstonecraft's trail has two purposes: to retrieve Imlay's lost treasure and hers. Her lost love.

One morning I put the breakfast things out on the table in the style of a magician's assistant, clear my throat, and announce "Girls. Look at this." They stop squabbling while I reverentially prop *Letters from Norway* up against the milk.

"Here's a mum who did lots of travelling, with her baby, hundreds of years ago."

Will reaches out to grab.

"Mary Wollstonecraft wrote an important book along the way, and she was secretly on a treasure hunt – NO Will, don't get porridge on her!"

"A *treasure hunt*? Is that why there's a boat?" They point at the stormy cover image.

"Yes. And she did all this ages ago, and she didn't have any family supporting her, or any teachers to help her."

"Like Ms Stevenson?"

"No, no one like Ms Stevenson. She had to teach herself, in a time when lots of people thought girls shouldn't even bother learning but just sit around being quiet."

They look at me blankly and before one of them has time to say "actually that sounds pretty cool" I hurry on: "It's like those Grimm stories we've been reading. Like a quest. She goes out into the world to try to fix something. But she meets all sorts of problems."

"Wizards disguised as a rook?"

"Not exactly."

"Does she marry a prince?"

"NO! I mean, no."

"And is there a happy ending?"

"Well, no."

On her departure, Wollstonecraft declares: "I am going to-wards the North in search of sunbeams!" On our departure, the enchanted and long-awaited day, I spring up at five o'clock and the sun is already up. I heave my rucksack on and pull my warm, reluctant baby from his cot. Off we set. In the airport queue I am reduced nearly to tears by the hateful rucksack. It's already killing me and we're still in bloody London. It is a vast, extending one with confusing straps all over, bought by Justin for one of his macho mountain trips. I have packed it badly; it sways away from me at the top, and if I lean down to Will in his buggy it lurches forward, hitting the back of my head. This can't be right.

But once we're on board I have the first "moment". A moment of pure triumph. I secretly smile. Will has fallen asleep and is perfectly arranged in a blanket on the seat next to me, limbs splayed out in the paradise of wanton baby sleep. One of his feet rests on my leg. His face looks fatter when he's asleep, his eyelashes rest on his cheeks.

I lean contentedly back, watching the small televisual aero-plane set out across the globe. I've always loved that plane. This one veers north, an intrepid direction, the obvious route being south. I bask in my contrary northerliness and breezily compare it to her eleven days on the rough seas from Hull to the Skagerrak.

Another self-congratulatory thrill comes with the solving of the "how to write" conundrum. Instead of a laptop, I've brought along a small Dictaphone. I pull it out of my bag now that he's asleep and have a furtive practice. The plan is to mumble into it, hands free, every time I have a thought. Those thoughts arrive right here on the page some time in the future, when I've got childcare.

We land in Gothenburg, Sweden. Gothenburg is where Wollstonecraft left her baby and the maid behind with some family friends, in preparation to undertake the next – more perilous – stage of the adventure alone. I've yet to find a friendly family I can dump Will with.

"Looks like I'm stuck with you then." I tell him.

He smiles. I smile back, tighten up the floppy, corpse-like rucksack and load us into our hire car.

The hire car is how I overcame the vexing problem of the five-hour mixture of buses and trains between the airport and the ferry. The problem that my friend found to be so very un-like *Touching the Void*. Not that that comment still rankles or anything.

So we drive up Sweden, listening to Swedish radio and look-ing at Swedish scenery. I chatter away to Will, who doesn't answer and is most probably asleep back there in his baby seat. I only just about managed to cram him into it – one of those little round ones like a half nutshell. His legs poke out, jumbled like a hermit crab. The landscape soars up on both sides of the road. It's still just like she says – there are fir trees and rocks everywhere. It's a landscape a child could draw: Christmas trees, zigzag mountain tops, box-shaped houses.

The trip in Wollstonecraft's determined footsteps leads us north from Gothenburg, up to Strömstad, which is where Wollstonecraft set sail. We too will embark here, taking the ferry over to Norway, then pressing onwards to Tønsberg, Risør and other places featuring Os with a line through them. I practise them out loud as I drive. But shortly before we reach Strömstad I get lost. We turn around and go back on ourselves. Will contributes nothing to my running commentary on where we went wrong. Surely this wouldn't happen with Wollstonecraft at the wheel. But hang on, maybe it does...

She's also heading north to Strömstad, but in an overnight horse-drawn coach. The other passengers are asleep. She stares out at the night summer sky of "clear softened blue". As she watches, the sun begins to rise, with "a kind of expectation that made me almost afraid to breathe, lest I should break the charm. I saw the sun – and sighed". Moments later the spell is further broken: a fellow passenger wakes and starts swearing at the driver. They've missed a turning and have to retrace their route. Unlike me, Wollstonecraft doesn't care. Despite having been up all night with her "orient beams" and "watery clouds", by the time they get to Strömstad she's bang up for it:

The wind had changed in the night, and my boat was ready. A dish of coffee and fresh linen recruited my spirits, and I directly set out again for Norway.

I love this woman. Relentless. Indomitable. And does that fresh linen bit mean that she changes her underwear? I have a coffee at Strömstad too, while we wait for our Norway-bound ferry.

I'm still in the same knickers though. But they're my best, saved out of the laundry especially for this momentous day. I inhale the coffee and her valour once more.

A dish of coffee and fresh linen recruited my spirits, and I directly set out again for Norway.

On board the Strömstad ferry is the most lavish buffet lunch I have ever attempted to ingest. With free booze. So by the time we totter up on deck to look for Norway, Will and I are feeling good. Very good. The ferry is white, with rows of orange lifeboats; the sky is a soft blue. The sea is flat, gently wrinkled by a breeze. The only whiteness on the sea is the wake of our boat. These are not the dark raging depths I had envisaged, but even so, the danger lurches inside me as we approach the railings. Will feels tiny. I gather him tight to my chest, his face in my neck, and sniff his thin baby hair.

Suddenly, there it is. A rocky, rocky coastline. Sharp intake of breath. I feel I recognize it: it's exactly as it should be. Tiny islands. Countless rocks poking above the sea. It doesn't look gentle. There's no sand: only bare rock. Distant layers of fir-tree-covered mountains on the horizon. I spot my first Norwegian house, a yellowy box balancing on a rock, and look around eagerly for someone I can point it out to. Look – an *actual Norwegian house*! But the people around us are Norwegians. They've come to do their household shopping more cheaply in Sweden. They've got their tartan wheely trollies loaded up with toilet roll, nappies and shampoo. I laugh out loud and hug Will to my chest again.

We set foot (my feet, Will's wheels) on Norway at seven o'clock in the evening, on the 8th of June. It's warm, the light is buttery golden, bits of white tree fluff drift down, backlit in the sunshine. Long shadows. We head across town and board the train for Tønsberg. I finally dare to count the remaining number of times that I will have to hoik the deadweight of rucksack on and off my back. Maybe it wasn't such a good idea to bring so many books. Rows of blood blisters now mark my upper arms. I decide that my baggage is emblematic. Wollstonecraft travelled with a broken heart, the victim of Imlay's infidelity. The rucksack is my tribute to her burden.

The train pulls in to Tønsberg at last. With the Rucksack of Piety on my back, and Will's buggy in front, I push onwards up the hill in search of our hostel. It's steep. I count back over the modes of transport we've ticked off today. I can't wait to reach the hostel. I get out of breath and wipe the sweat from my face. Then I get lost and come back down the hill. I ask a man in a car where the hostel is. He tells us to go back up the hill. It's still sunny and very hot. Will rubs his eyes and starts to cry. I want to cry too. I begin to swear out loud. *Touching the Void* my arse.

The next morning Will and I wake up in fairy-tale land. I'm in a little wooden bunk bed, top bunk. He's in a cot with embroidered sheets depicting a lamb in a bonnet. It's nine o'clock, and we've both slept a ton. I give thanks to the parents' supreme deity, the god of sleep, that Will didn't hassle me in the night. We stretch and smile at each other. We go for breakfast in a white room full of frilly old furniture. It's charming – jam in quaint unmatching bowls, creamy honey, perfect bread. White eggs in a basket. The kind of food that Little Red Riding Hood took to her granny.

Tønsberg is a pretty coastal town to the south of Oslo, a jumble of many-coloured wooden houses that look like attractive garden sheds. Wollstonecraft loves it here. She makes this the base for her treasure-hunting ventures. Here she gathers herself together. She begins to recover from life as a destitute foreign single mum living in the French Reign of Terror, and from her attempted suicide.

Wollstonecraft enthuses about the humanity of Norway's justice system, calls Norway "the most free community I have ever observed", and relates a number of odd local legends, adding that she has "formed a very just opinion of the character of the Norwegians, without being able to hold converse with them". She praises their "artless kindness" and dishes out counsel to farmers on how they should be selling their produce, and mothers on how they should be bringing up their kids. She learns to row, swims in the sea, drinks the local well-water and begins to feel "renovated".

Wollstonecraft never sits still for long. Between the bouts of observing, writing and lecturing, she's forever shooting off "over hedge and ditch" on bracing walks. I want just to potter, amble, daydream in her restless onwards steps. And unlike her, I doubt very much that we'll be going for a swim today. Cold rain is pouring insistently out of a dark sky. I tuck the plastic rain-shelter bubble over Will's buggy and borrow an umbrella from the hostel.

We're meeting Ursula Houge, Tønsberg's eminent historical tour guide. She will take us to the places where Wollstonecraft relaxed, posted off her stream of unhappy letters to Imlay and dined out with Tønsberg's finest. Ursula has white hair in a bob, the correct clothing for Norwegian weather, and appropriate shoes. She zooms up the hill at a fair old clip, throwing out historical facts left and right.

Will and I try to keep up. His buggy is stupidly large, one of those off-road things. I brought it because it doubles as a bed. And this is exactly what it feels like: pushing a bed uphill. But as we push upwards we make a fortunate discovery. It turns out that our hostel on the hill, chosen purely for economic reasons, sits immediately below Wollstonecraft's favourite spot.

This is not just any old hill. Tønsberg is the oldest town in Norway. And here, looming over us amid some older ruins, is a tower called the Slottsfjellet. It's more good-looking than it sounds. The ancient royal Ynglings lived here in the first millennium, and King Haakon Haakonsson fought off the Danes here in 1253. This site has seen centuries of battles, sieges, fortifications, royal weddings and deaths, before it became the favourite private dreaming place for a philosopher who wanted to make the world better but couldn't sort out her own life. And now us. Polite people walking round in circles in the endless rain. We've found her place. Right here, Wollstonecraft sits and writes, overlooking the town and the surrounding sea:

...the white sails as turned the cliffs, or seemed to take shelter under the pines which covered the little islands that so gracefully rose to render the terrific ocean beautiful. The fishermen were calmly casting their nets; whilst the seagulls hovered over the unruffled deep.

This is still the scene today. Apart from it's chucking it down, the rain is now so hard it's bouncing back up. We walk round and round the top of the hill. After a bit of squawking, Will falls asleep inside his bubble as we huddle under our umbrellas. We stand lost in conversation as the water splashes around us, and Ursula sets Wollstonecraft's political observations in a Norwegian setting. Far below, a large ferry comes in, leaving a trail on the grey sea.

I mention that the words Wollstonecraft uses most often about Norway are "independent", "sprightly" and "industrious". "We do like hard work," says Ursula. "It matters to us." She talks about equality and financial independence, proud of her enlightened country. She tells me that couples always split a restaurant bill. This would have meant everything to Wollstonecraft:

Independence I have long considered as the grand blessing of life, the basis of every virtue, and independence I will ever secure by contracting my wants, though I were to live on a barren heath.

"And she's right," says Ursula. "It's good to be financially independent. And generally, when you are married, it's quite usual that a couple will have one bank account for all the household bills and everything, but you would also have your own private bank account. My husband was exceptionally kind about things like that—"

Ursula looks away towards the sea. We are close together under the umbrellas, but I lean towards her. She is crying.

"I lost him a year ago yesterday."

I ask what his name was. He was called Per. She waves away my proffered tissue, pulling out her own handkerchief. We manage to laugh about his very typical Norwegian name. She blows her nose, exclaims "So so!", and we carry on talking about Wollstonecraft and independence.

Eventually we head back down the hill to shelter from the rain in a café, with black coffees and cake. We carry on through town, taking in the grander houses. Here's where Wollstone-craft mingled with the Mayor and other people of influence, gathering public support in her hunt for the last-known person to see Imlay's missing silver: Captain Peder Ellefsen.

We walk through puddles back to the hostel, where the owner, who knows Ursula, brings over a tray with tea and thin slices of cheese on rye bread.

"Nice walk in the rain?"

"Ja," says Ursula. "We covered some important ground."

She smiles at me, I smile back, my mouth full of Jarls-berg. I hear a strangled cry and leap up just in time to wrest the hostel owner's cat's tail from the hands of my beaming son.

Later in the afternoon the rain stops, its absence suddenly au-dible. I seize the moment to go back up onto Wollstonecraft's favourite hill. I pop Will into his chaise longue on wheels, and we barrel back up the steep slopes through the dripping grass. The birds are singing all around, also relieved by a break from the rain. I have to sit here for a while, in Wollstonecraft's secret resting place. This is a privilege. There's no one else around. The darkest clouds have lifted, but it's still misty. I perch on a large stone, gently bring out my copy of *Letters from Norway* and read some passages aloud.

> *Here I have frequently strayed, sovereign of the waste; I seldom met any human creature – and sometimes, reclining on the mossy down, under the shelter of a rock, the prattling of the sea amongst the pebbles has lulled me to sleep...*
>
> *You have sometimes wondered, my dear friend, at the extreme affection of my nature – but such is the temperature of my soul... For years have I endeavoured to calm an impetuous tide... It was striving against the stream – I must love and admire with warmth, or I sink into sadness.*

This dreamy interlude wandering into a defence of her implacable manner is a direct plea to her lover, the unnamed "dear friend". He's there, always. It's impossible to forget that she's trying to win Imlay back. Wollstonecraft loved just as she lived: passionately, and at a hundred miles an hour – as if it was the last day of her life. If she'd had the technology, she'd easily have sent a dozen reproachful text messages a minute. In capitals.

I want to be Wollstonecraft's companion, but I feel incapable of her depths and her restless energy. Her bleak shuddering sighs are echoed only by my contented ones. Above all, there's the inescapable fact that she tried (more than once) to kill herself. While I can't quite shake it off, I'm afraid to approach the theme. Her many detractors have used Wollstonecraft's attempted suicides as proof of bad character, or wheeled out the creaky old "undermining her legacy" attack, so naturally I'm compelled to defend her. But how? I've tried to ignore them, to gloss over them. But here, in the misty air, I can almost sense her sadness – the neediness between the lines – clutching on to me as I read.

Guiltily I lift myself out of her words for a breather, trying to imagine how her smashed-in hopes took her to that brink. It fails: I fail to sink into her sadness. "Thinking of death makes us tenderly cling to our affections – with more than usual tenderness," she writes, later adding: "It appears to me impossible that I should cease to exist ... Surely something resides in this heart that is not perishable – and life is more than a dream."

She loved her child, and made "precautions" for her care. But she still did it. She tried to die. I look at Will. He's humming to himself. She didn't love her little Frances any less than this. I sit for more long minutes on that stone, in a deep vague sadness, getting a damp bum while Will grabs out for the long grasses waving nearby. I look around again. Above all, above the sea and the town, it's so peaceful. There's a sense of healthiness here: it feels wholesome and sane. It could be the cleanliness, or the proximity of the sea, but I can see why it was here that Wollstonecraft began to recover. Eventually I sigh out a long breath, and inside my head I tell her something:

You haven't ceased to exist.

Chapter Four

"Sympathy in a Strange Land"

When we get back to the hostel, Will invents a new game. He crawls at high speed out of our room and away down a long corridor. I wait, then chase after him, scoop him up and bring him, laughing, back in my arms. Off he crawls again, his hands make a splat-splat noise on the floor, a light clapping, as he trundles like a determined beetle. We do this until he gets tired, and I start to think about packing up the monster rucksack.

Moving on we have yet to meet Gunnar, the tireless Wollstonecraft detective. Mick, the heartbroken captain in a stripy sailor's top. Knut, the only communist mayor in Norway, who is proud that Wollstonecraft came to his town, despite the fact that she detested it. I will encounter a taste of what proper fans get when they meet another fan. It's solidarity with a slight edge: "I love and understand her." "I love her more. I loved her first!" "Well, I am so intimate that I can criticize her – we're practically siblings."

But first, like Wollstonecraft, we must head west. Wollstonecraft left Tønsberg having enlisted the great and the good to her cause. She put together a legal case and was lobbying hard. Urged on by Imlay, her strategy was to impress upon Norwegians that their fellow countryman, Peder Ellefsen, was a tarnish upon their reputation. She would take it to the highest authorities. But first she must track him down and confront him face to face. "I am forewarned that I shall find them still more cunning and fraudulent as I advance towards the westward". She pursues Ellefsen westward along the crazy shoreline. And we pursue her.

At the bus station in Tønsberg they tell me we'll have to change buses twice on the way to our next stop, Kragerø. But it's not as bad as I expect. Luckily the buses are a feature of child-friendly Norway: the drivers leap out to help us on board. They smile and chat. One holds Will while I fold the buggy and then asks his passengers to move, giving us two seats together. I'm still recovering from the contrast to British buses when he even installs a baby seat, so Will can sleep all the way.

It's another moment of triumph. I've found that, on balance, travelling with Will is proving to make life easier rather than harder. He gives me the biggest smile when we're in the queue at the bus station, and I'm instantly happier than anyone else in the whole place. I realize that at home I'm always trying to squeeze my life around him. It's like a see-saw, either doing baby things or grown-up things, but never both.

But this is different. Here we are on the same side, in it together. I tell him everything that's happening, and he smiles back. Even if it's about how I'm dying for the loo and should've gone before we left, he beams at me. I reach into his baby seat, stroke his see-through blonde hair and gently twirl the curls around his ears.

Travelling with a baby is especially handy for anyone of a curious bent. It gives you improved access, a licence to talk to anyone you like. People catch your eye and smile. (Some people do hate kids, but they probably also hate humanity and are therefore no loss.) Will's presence elicits acts of kindness I'd surely have otherwise missed. Maybe I look more vulnerable. Wollstonecraft remarks on the Norwegians' curiosity towards her:

> *A woman, coming alone, interested them. And I know not whether my weariness gave me a look of peculiar delicacy; but they approached to assist me and enquire after my wants, as if they were afraid to hurt and wished to protect me. The sympathy I inspired, thus dropping down from the clouds in a strange land, affected me…*

A young couple on the bus waves at Will and strikes up conversation with me. They've dropped down from the clouds in Sweden, and are travelling to Kragerø to look for work. They tell me many young Swedes are coming to Norway now, because unemployment is higher there, and wages are higher here. They offer Will some radioactive-looking sweets, and he munches them while I try to look mellow and un-disapproving.

There are wild lupins everywhere, alongside the railways, roads and motorways. Bushes of towering purple spires, giving a crazy Moominland vibe. Another person on the bus tells me it has now been made an offence to plant lupins in your garden, because they all escaped and are taking over the entire country. This can't be true, but I love it anyway. Heading towards Kragerø, the landscape through the bus windows changes dramatically. It gets wilder, steeper soaring rocks. Road signs feature pictures of a moose. Our road hugs the coastline, so nothing is in a straight line, as the water comes in and out of the land. It dominates our route, sending us over and around.

I pull out my huge map of Norway, folded specially to the right place. This is not a country that fits easily onto a map, being quite a silly shape, like Chile. Norway is like a large hairy blanket draped over the top of Europe. Looking closer, you see that the country is almost all coast: endless islands, zigzag coastlines and fjords inside fjords. There is water everywhere. I recall reading that eighty per cent of Norwegians live within ten kilometres of salt water. It is their element. Rocks burst through all around us, small islands, soaring rocky cliffs, or the tell-tale white foam showing that they're just below the water's surface.

I rest my forehead against the windowpane, and another blaze of purple lupins zooms by. I'm not entirely sure what the next part of our journey will entail. It's all up in the air. But of one thing I'm certain: of all the pieces of good fortune I've had so far on this trip – a gleefully large number when I think about it – the best must have been making contact with Gunnar Molden.

Gunnar is a Norwegian historian, museum curator and Wollstonecraft enthusiast. His research into the treacherous tale of Wollstonecraft and the missing silver spans decades and countries. Among his discoveries is a letter written by Wollstonecraft herself, buried for years in some maritime archives in Denmark. His detective work informs the thrilling 'Silver Ship' chapter of the Lyndall Gordon biography that I've been devouring.

I first contacted him by email, expressing my interest in Wollstonecraft's voyage. He replied politely, including his phone number in case I had any questions. Are you kidding? Of course I did – I called him right away. He was quiet and shy, and full of Wollstonecraft knowledge. On and off, through the many swerves and obstacles of getting the trip organized, he has regularly helped out and given contacts and ideas. He is the fairy godfather of my trip. And I've never actually met him.

Now we're on a bus to Kragerø where Gunnar has asked his cousin Ingvild and her husband Per to put us up in their summer house. The plan is to stay there for a night and then set off on the boat trip the following morning. The boat trip. The Boat Trip. This is the maximum, the ultimate, the most Wollstonecrafty part of my journey. We plan to travel by boat just the way Wollstonecraft did, right up to her final and most westerly destination: Risør. Just as it is in her letters.

I'm struggling to believe the boat-trip part: it's a bit too good to be true. Gunnar says he's sorted it out. I told him, way back, that I couldn't afford to pay him as a consultant, and he dismissed the idea: "Leave it to me. And I can find us a boat." Wollstonecraft met similar generosity:

The farmers are hospitable as well as independent. Offering once to pay for some coffee I drank when taking shelter from the rain, I was asked, rather angrily, if a little coffee was worth paying for.

A little coffee these days will set you back around £5. In a country where you have to double-check your finances before you order a drink, how I've managed to access a whole boat is still a mystery to me.

Who, among the people at the bus station in Kragerø, is cousin Ingvild? I have no idea what she looks like, but fortunately we are fairly easy to spot. No one else is tottering under a rucksack like a misshapen tortoise whilst pushing a beaming baby in a large buggy. Ingvild comes up and gives me a hug. We chat as we walk over a bridge and up the extremely steep hill to her house. Good god! This whole country is on a slope of about one in three. I try not to pant as I speak.

By the time I have emerged from under the rucksack and released Will from the buggy to crawl straight up the nearest rock, Ingvild has brought out the best tray I've ever seen. White bread and poppyseed bread, butter, fresh slices of raw salmon, a pot of apricot jam and two mugs of steaming black coffee. I'm starving. I set to, while Ingvild hovers over Will, singing to him in Norwegian as he tries out some rock climbing. I cradle the coffee cup, breathing into it and letting the steam blur my vision. This is going to be a good place to stay.

Ingvild and Per are generous hosts. Wollstonecraft would've loved this: staying in real people's houses rather than inns and hostels. We eat fish and talk about Norway. Per is director of the National Maritime Museum in Oslo. Again – the watery theme. He tells me how Kragerø used to provide the wider world with ice.

From the 1820s, tons of pure Norwegian ice were shipped abroad to be stored in ice wells, and used for medical and food-preservation purposes. Eventually Kragerø's finest came to the attention of one of London's most life-enhancing immigrants.

Carlo Gatti was the granddaddy of ice cream: his penny ices gave a taste of previously unimaginable joy to the ordinary people of London. I smile and ruffle Will's head. Londoners were lapping up Kragerø long before we got here.

There's a slight pause in the aquatic chat, and I'm suddenly sleepy. Using Will as an excuse for an early night, we head upstairs. Ingvild has kindly pushed two beds together in the attic room, but there's no cot. Despite being hobbled by the faded-pink sleeping bag handed down from his sisters, Will begins to romp. This free-range set-up is a novelty for him: he clambers all over, pulling my hair, tapping the walls, chuckling. In the middle of the night I despair and tie a blanket round his middle, then tuck both ends firmly in between the mattresses. He battles this cruel anchor at some length before we finally sleep.

Early the next morning I'm walking back down the steep hill, half-dragged by Will in his weighty vehicle, to get nappies from the shop. After a rough night, Will is now embarking on a high-maintenance morning. He keeps shaking his head from side to side and looking affronted. "I'm the one who should be affronted, mate." I refer him to the nappy containing a monstrous poo that I've just disposed of in Ingvild's polite wooden house. Such an unruly beast that I had to double-bag, then bury it at the bottom of their bin. We continue down the hill in an atmosphere of mutual resentment.

The tyranny of Will means I still haven't brushed my teeth, showered or had breakfast. It's a big and important day – the long-awaited day of the boat trip, and my first meeting with Gunnar. And I'm starting it with a headache, dry eyes and tetchy feelings. These extend to Wollstonecraft. Won't she just once mention what a monumental pain in the neck children can be? It's all "blessed darling babe" this, and "rosy cheeks" that. Why? Because she's got a maid. She has Marguerite. I do not have Marguerite. I catch my reflection in a fish shop window, scowling.

On our return, Ingvild offers to take Will while I gratefully shower and get dressed. I join them for a miracle fry-up. A few fried eggs later things are looking up in Kragerø and we're raring to go. Wollstonecraft herself never came here, but a house that she stayed in did. Norwegian houses apparently travel around in the most light-hearted way. I find this funny, coming from a land of sturdy bricks, with our tales of pigs who build straw houses. And look what happened to them. "But it's simple!" says Ingvild. "You just pack it up. You take the house down plank by plank – they're numbered. And then you put it all back up somewhere else." Well, there's the global Scandi phenomena of Lego and Ikea explained.

Shortly after breakfast, Gunnar Molden arrives. Here at last: the great Wollstonecraft detective. I hadn't put a face on him in my mind – perhaps someone wizened and wispy-looking. But he's younger than I expected, and quite solid. He looks like a boy scout on a day trip, carrying two plastic bags and a rucksack, with a baseball cap pulled down firmly over his eyes. He has a determined expression and he's not very talkative.

Ingvild's husband Per joins us, and we set off to look for the Wollstonecraft house that moved from somewhere else to here. We knock on the door. The owner is an attractive yoga teacher. She has never heard of Wollstonecraft, nor had any idea that anyone of great historical importance lived in her house. She kindly offers to hold Will while we look around inside. No way! He's coming right in with me.

We stand around inside the house, looking at the wooden planks. Gunnar and Per chat to each other, while I roam eagerly about, examining her stairway, trying to get a vibe, like some hapless Ghostbuster – a hint, an echo, a *feeling* of anything that could tell me that Wollstonecraft was truly here. It doesn't happen. Yoga Lady's house is style-magazine trendy, with art books and vases just so. By the time I catch myself poking around in her bathroom cabinet, it's clear that this is not working, and I trundle back downstairs, Will on my hip, to rejoin Per and Gunnar.

They're still standing there, talking in detail about the house's wooden panelling. On top of the failed ghost-busting I confess I'd expected a more immediate bond with Gunnar, given our shared passion. I slyly observe him talking, and he's so low-key he's hardly even there. What could possibly have drawn him to one of history's most shouty women? I resolve to find out. This may take time. Not least because Norwegians talk so slowly.

After years working in radio I can't help but to hear this kind of speech with a sinking heart: "This will take ages to de-umm." De-umming is a self-explanatory part of a radio producer's job. A bad ummer means your interview can be minutes shorter once it's been de-ummed. Of course you mustn't get carried away, you don't want someone to sound completely different. And on rare occasions an umm is a powerful signifier of deliberation or discomfort. This should never be de-ummed.

But despite the deliberate slowness (new layers of rudeness here, on top of Wollstonecraft's centuries-old ones), the Norwegian language itself is delightful. It sounds like German being spoken in a Welsh accent. Norwegians have a strange vocal tic: they say "ja" *inwardly*. It's a small gasp of incoming breath, designed for agreeing politely or filling a pause. The first time I notice it is with Gunnar, and I wonder if he's suffering a respiratory difficulty. I soon begin trying it out when no one else is around.

We say goodbye to Yoga Lady, impressing on her, one last time, how her house is truly blessed by the greatness of its possible former inhabitant. She nods patiently. We head off down towards the harbour, and on the way we bump into a distinguished whiskery old chap who is greeted by Per and Gunnar with some degree of reverence. He is a retired historian. Per and Gunnar introduce me as a person from London who is writing a book.

"What's it about?" he says peering into my face.

"It's inspired by the life of Mary Wollstonecraft," I say.

"Ah yes – that Wollstonecraft. I've read her and I didn't like her," he says. "She's one of those feminist types, all her writing is just a load of emotions."

I'm stunned. I know of course that people don't like her. In history she has been despised, slandered, rejected from all sides. I know this. But after so much fan-club action I'm unprepared, and too slow to gather my wits in her defence:

"But – but, there are lots of, you know, facts too!"

Afterwards I'm ruffled, I've let her down. As we walk away, the indignation grows. After all, she writes about Reason all the time. But even so, should there really be no emotion? Emotions have their uses: "We reason deeply, when we forcibly feel!" And anyway, who wouldn't get emotional, surrounded by dismissive entitled old farts LIKE YOU? I retrospectively crack my mind's knuckles. Yeah. He got off lightly.

Gunnar and I say goodbye to Per and continue down to the harbour to find Mick. He is the skipper of the boat we'll be travelling in, and a well-known local figure. He's originally English, but moved to Norway decades ago. Mick has a stripy maritime top and a cockney accent; he's tall with white bristles all over his face and head. He has crinkles around his eyes from staring at distant blue horizons. He is the most perfect specimen of a sea captain you could ever wish for. He also plays bluegrass banjo and has a broken heart, I discover within a few moments of meeting him.

"This boat is a Colin Archer!" Gunnar announces while Mick beams with pride.

"Ah, a Colin Archer," I say politely.

"A Colin Archer, yes, a genuine Colin Archer," they repeat with joy. It turns out that Colin Archer was a nineteenth-century Norwegian shipbuilder of Scottish descent who became a national hero. He designed the nation's fleet of lifeboats and built the mighty *Fram*, sailed by both Nansen and Amundsen on their legendary polar expeditions. The same Nansen who invented the Nansen Passport for stateless refugees. As a quietly huge gift to the world, this almost beats Kragerø's ice cream.

"You are safer in a Colin Archer than in any other boat!" shouts Mick, as we hoist my rucksack and Will's buggy on board. I have a fleeting recollection that the same was said of the *Titanic*, but this is indeed a powerful-looking boat. "This is my girl!" he booms. "After my wife left me, the boat is all I have. She's thirty-two foot long, weighs eleven tons, and her average speed is five to six knots depending on the wind."

She is called *Anjava*, and we're finally all aboard her sturdy deck. I freely adopt the gendered sailor-speak, now that I can talk about Colin Archers with confidence. I feel positively seaworthy. The engine roars into life, then settles to a steady chug, and there's the satisfying smell of diesel. And off we set: Mick the skipper, Gunnar the detective, and me and Will, on the soaring wooden decks of the redoubtable *Anjava*.

This is the most anticipated day. We are hot on the trail. This part of the journey was huge for Wollstonecraft: she had left Tønsberg and was making her way by sea to Risør. So far she has been doing all she can to gather support for her cause, but at Risør she will actually meet the captain, face to face, in a showdown that could change everything. Her fortunes are in the balance. The wind is in my face. I'm gulping down the excitement of joining her, here, and in the lines of the book.

Chapter Five

"In a Little Boat upon the Ocean"

The sun is dazzling, the whole sky is bright. The joy I feel as we slice through the clear waters is irrepressible like laughter. I am smiling away like an idiot. "Wow!" I shout, pointing out a large jellyfish. The muted response from the others indicates that this is a common and uninteresting sight. But I remember Wollstonecraft writing about them, I whip out the book and find the reference. She confusingly calls them starfish, adding:

> They look like thickened water, with a white edge – and four purple circles, of different forms, were in the middle, over an incredible number of fibres, or white lines. Touching them, the cloudy substance would turn or close, first on one side, then on the other, very gracefully; but when I took one of them up in the ladle with which I heaved the water out of the boat, it appeared only a colourless jelly.

Her love of wildness and nature is clear. But I can't help laughing at the idea of the great founder of feminism hoiking a jellyfish out of the sea and prodding at it like a kid.

Leaving the harbour, we look back to Kragerø, and can just make out the figure of Ingvild behind the house we stayed in last night. She waves from high up on the rocks. We wave back. I feel so intrepid I keep catching my breath. Gunnar brings out a paper bag full of cinnamon buns, spiralled with sugar, and we stuff them greedily into our mouths.

Leaving Kragerø is not plain sailing. You keep going for miles, past more and ever more islands, unsure which is mainland and which is not, at sea but not properly out at sea. Finally there is the last island, Jomfruland. In full factual mode and using no emotions whatsoever, Wollstonecraft reports, translating its name:

> One of the islands, called Virgin Land, is a flat, with some depth of earth, extending for half a Norwegian mile, with three farms on it, tolerably well cultivated."

No farms there today, just seagulls. I look one in the eye and wonder if its ancestor saw her pass by. With this stern outpost of land behind us, we are finally out and away from the reaches of the rocky coastline. It feels different. The swell is much deeper, the spray flies higher. *Anjava* is properly at work now, her gleaming sides dominate the water. Will is still in the buggy, wrapped up warm and dozing. I realize I'd completely forgotten about him, and guiltily sniff him to check the state of his nappy. All clear.

There is so much to see in every direction – the wind chasing the birds along the skyline, the myriad rocks and islands rising all around. The idea of these being the peaks of some dark, undersea mountains makes my guts lurch. I feel vulnerable, even in a Colin Archer, and I wonder what Wollstonecraft's vessel was like, as she sailed these spiky shores, past "straggling houses" on "shivering rocks". She writes:

Though we were in the open sea, we sailed more amongst the rocks and islands than in my passage from Strömstad; and they often formed very picturesque combinations. Few of the high ridges were entirely bare; the seeds of some pines or firs had been wafted by the winds or waves, and they stood to brave the elements.

Always unconventional, Wollstonecraft is celebrating the wildness here: this land untamed and unaltered by mankind. She then adds herself to the picture:

Sitting then in a little boat on the ocean, amidst strangers, with sorrow and care pressing hard on me – buffeting me about from clime to clime.

Here she has something in common with Mick, who's moved from examining the map to telling tales of love gone wrong. Mick keeps correcting himself: "My wife... my *ex*-wife" – about how they fell in love, they lived on boats, they travelled the world, they were together for twenty-three years. But she grew away, she wanted something else. "She said she wanted some time out. I should've noticed, I should've seen it coming." But he didn't. "I was totally gutted. I'm gradually getting back on my feet, after six years."

He says he still can't believe that she's gone. It's hard to know what to say to a heartbroken sea captain. I want to tell him about Wollstonecraft's heartbreak, only it doesn't seem helpful. Just then Gunnar the dark horse unexpectedly joins in, with some tales of his own. A disastrous love affair, a new romance when he least expected it; love at first sight with a wonderful woman. They now have two young children. "But I'm too old for this; I had a crisis when I was fifty-five that I was too old to be doing this."

A tender moment between a salty sea dog and an introverted historian, afloat at sea, is the last thing I'd expected. I'm managing with some difficulty to contain my regular exclamations on the completely fantastic, amazing brilliance of the sea, the sky, the jellyfish, the boat, the cinnamon buns. I sit in unusual silence, the map and the book propped on my knees, while they unburden their hearts.

Wollstonecraft praises Norwegian pilots as being the best in the world. And they certainly had to be:

> *I soon perceived that an experienced mariner was necessary to guide us, for we were continually obliged to tack about to avoid the rocks – which, scarcely reaching to the surface of the water, could only be discovered by the breaking of the waves over them.*

The pilots lived in small houses dotting the islands, and earned a living by guiding passing vessels through the rocks and round the shores. It was a competitive business: pilots would all rush out to an approaching ship, and the first one to get there would fling himself aboard, thereby claiming the reward of steering it around. His abandoned boat would then be brought back in, sometimes by his children. It wasn't uncommon for pilots to die attempting to throw themselves on board.

Human frailty in the face of these fierce, wild shores affects Wollstonecraft deeply, but it's not only herself she pities. She begins to spin out a thread of thought revealing her love for humanity, and her curious mind at its best. Wollstonecraft is inspired to imagine a future, a couple of million years hence, when earth would be

> *so completely peopled as to render it necessary to inhabit every spot – yes: these bleak shores. Imagination went still farther, and pictured the state of man when the earth could no longer support him. Where was he to fly from universal famine? Do not smile: I really became distressed for these fellow creatures, yet unborn.*

It's not for another few years that the man whose name has become shorthand for over-population, Thomas Robert Malthus, visits this part of the world. In 1799 he visits with the travel writer Edward Daniel Clarke, who, as it happens, is reading *Letters from Norway*. Around the same time, Malthus publishes his famous book, *An Essay on the Principle of Population*. In it, he argues that continued population growth will lead to poverty and famine. Once again, our gal Wolly is ahead of the curve.

She hopes to press onwards to Risør, but her journey is broken sooner than she expects. Darkness and bad weather force them ashore at a tiny place called Portør. "It is indeed a corner of the world," she writes. And it's here that we plan to make our first stop of the day. I think back to reading about Portør at home, and how long it took me to find it on the map. It is a miniscule coastal fleck, dwarfed even by the letters of its own name. Mick jumps to his feet as we approach. Passing a number of islands, through a tiny channel into a natural harbour, we find the modest cluster of wooden houses that is Portør.

The miracle of approaching land on a boat is how the world gradually returns itself to you. The land comes into focus, revealing itself bit by bit until suddenly there you are, about to leave the floating existence and become solid, normal again. It's dull to be standing on earth once more, I feel stunted. Like rushing off the end of an airport travelator, abruptly back on your own disappointing legs.

We moor up – and there on the jetty is a striking woman. She's a "local person of interest" that Per thought we should meet. Her name is Grethe Rønning Clausen; she is tanned, elegantly dressed and glamorous. She could be about seventy or eighty, but somehow I couldn't possibly ask. Grethe offers us black coffee and princess cake, an oversized vanilla sponge in the shape of a flower, drizzled with icing. Will clasps a chunk in his hands, and I carry him in my arms as we all wander about.

Portør is tiny and bright. The sea is encircled by round soaring rocks, smooth enough to walk up – indeed they invite you. Wollstonecraft ends part of her letter here saying "Adieu! I must trip up the rocks". The hill-like rocks have pockets of moss, tufted grass and wild flowers. Several perfectly round holes in the surface near the top have become bright puddles reflecting the sky. A lookout post clings to the upper slopes, from which the pilots would keep watch, staring out on the sea all around.

Next door to Grethe's house is a small green lawn that was the original site of the place we visited at this morning, the portable house that came from Portør to Kragerø to be lived in centuries later by Yoga Lady. Mick is clearly taken by Grethe, and they fall into maritime reminiscences. When she was young she would sail to Kragerø, bringing the pilot boat back on her own. Grethe has a quiet voice, and when we settle down so I can record her, Mick keeps bursting in and talking about his boat, and Will crawls around exclaiming, and seagulls shriek overhead. I lean in closer as she begins her tale:

"We were from different regions of Norway. Everyone said it wouldn't last, for we were so different. But I loved him from the first time I saw him. It was a festival day in Norway. There was a fair, and I saw someone arriving on a boat, a very nice boy, but I didn't talk to him. That night there was a party with dancing. I went along with my girl friend from school, and she had on a red suit with pearls. And that special young man, he always got to dance with her."

Grethe's blue eyes twinkle: this story has the feel of a favourite. She enjoys her audience, and we're all captivated.

"I said to my mum: I don't think it's nice here and I want to go home. I stood beside this girl, and we saw him coming back, and I said to her, now he's coming to dance with you again. But then he saw me. And I saw him. And yes, that was it: done. The first thing he said to me was, had I changed my shoes? I said yes, it was too warm. We'd never talked before, but he had noticed me. We started dancing. I was only seventeen years old. It was a beautiful spring."

The special young man who arrived on a boat was a seventh-generation pilot from Portør, and Grethe married him and came here to live with him.

"The life of pilots was so hard and dangerous. Seven pilots lived here in Portør, and they had to compete for work. As you know, the first person on board the ship got the job. One time my husband's uncle, also a pilot, knew that a ship was coming that night. He had placed his clothes by the bed when he slept, so that he could be the first one up. When he got up he leapt into his wife's clothes by accident. But he still got the job!"

Grethe has not only heard of Wollstonecraft, she brings out her own copy – an old hardback edition of *Letters from Norway* in Norwegian.

"It's very nice," she says, flicking through the pages. "She had to be strong at the time, hundreds of years ago. I can't imagine how she could make it, and with a little child too."

The bare wildness of the surrounding land is in stark contrast with the inside of Grethe's home. It's a special place. Photos of generations of smiling children cover the walls; her house is bustling with lace curtains, chandeliers and trinkets. One windowsill alone is populated by two bowls of flowers placed on lace doilies, a miniature gas lamp, two sailor figurines standing next to a china lighthouse, three china cockerels, a yellow duckling wearing a flower necklace, a white jug and two sleeping china babies.

It's hard not to feel a strong affection for Portør. Wollstonecraft sleeps well in what she calls this "little haven", and she dreams about baby Frances, left behind:

My little cherub was again hiding her face in my bosom. I heard her sweet cooing beat on my heart from the cliffs, and I saw her tiny footsteps on the sands.

She feels unusually content here, despite the dangerous weather they've fled and the darkness of the mission ahead. She seems surprised, even caught out by her own tranquillity: "Let me catch pleasure on the wing – I may be melancholy tomorrow." These dreamt tiny footsteps make me turn towards the retreating figure of Will with extra love, recalling the painful spike of imagining an absent child. Wollstonecraft moves on to the "cleanliness and comfort of the dwelling". Her landlady, just like Grethe, has "individual taste". Wollstonecraft rather ungraciously adds: "they live here very cheap ... I suspect, by their furniture, that they smuggle a little."

Portør is magical, but like our heroine I'm anxious to press on for Risør. We take our leave of Grethe, waving as we adjust to being back on board the *Anjava*. I carry on waving for a bit longer than is necessary, as the kindly haven of Portør slips away from us. We push on, back out into the open sea. Everyone falls quiet. Something about being out at sea makes me want to freeze time: I don't want this to end. It's more windy now, and the sky has darkened to a deeper blue.

We've been purposefully at sea for some time when a strange thing happens. Suddenly the engine cuts out and the boat begins to lurch. Mick shouts "Don't panic!" and springs up, hastily putting up the sails and running around the decks. We're doubly shocked: first the sudden absence of the engine noise, then the rocking. It's as though we have turned from a Colin Archer into a mere cork, bobbing on top of the waves.

I go below deck holding Will tight, passing him to Gunnar as I unfold his buggy and put the brake on. It's idiotic to be faffing with a buggy while the boat plunges from side to side, but at least it's something to do. Gunnar has gone shiny and grey, and says he's feeling seasick. I take Will off him and, struggling to keep my feet firmly planted, strap him into the buggy. Cupboard doors start to swing and crash; the movement is surprisingly violent.

I admit to myself that this is most definitely scary. The stupidity of boats presents itself with force: water isn't where humans are meant to be. *Anjava* may well be far superior to Wollstonecraft's vessel, but the sea is still the sea. The movement is all wild and wrong. Things roll out of cupboards, the cutlery swings and crashes around, the curtains flap outwards: it's like a poltergeist scene from a cheap horror movie. Up on deck, Mick has cut his hand and is bleeding. As he hoists the sails, he shouts that without the engine we can't go on: we are against the wind. We can't go on to Risør, but will be blown back the way we came.

Then, just as inexplicably, the engine restarts and we are jolted back into action. No one knows why. Mick looks annoyed not to have an explanation; he chunters for a while about air bubbles in the fuel. We settle back into our places up on deck. No one admits how frightening it was. The sea has reminded us who's boss, but we're still afloat, and we're still heading for Risør. I feel a renewed love for *Anjava* and a nauseous gratitude. I'm beginning to understand why people develop such personal relationships with their boats.

Gunnar's face resumes its normal colour, and he holds Will in his arms. He looks so gentle holding Will, I can't help staring. It is strange to see someone holding someone that you love – it's almost a form of intimacy. Gunnar's face seems to express something deep. Unsure why I feel the need to dispel the moment, I make a banal comment about babies being excellent hot-water bottles. Will looks over at me, and his eyes are deep blue like the blueness all around. He rubs his face, then without any protest he falls asleep right there on Gunnar's chest.

Onwards to Risør, I am buoyed up by the mini-drama of the temperamental boat on the high seas. It feeds into the thrill of our imminent arrival in Risør. What will it look like? What will we find? Mick and Gunnar will leave us here and head back home. I feel clingy, as though we all belong together. I don't want it to be over. Is this what happens on boats – the interdependence, the team-building thing? Maybe I'm tired and cold, and in truth, perhaps a bit nervous. The next leg of the journey, after all, is the place that Wollstonecraft absolutely hated.

Risør is the westernmost point of Wollstonecraft's journey. This small town is hugely important: she will meet Captain Peder Ellefsen here and challenge him about the missing silver. Her success depends on the outcome of this meeting: this is her chance to prove herself and regain Imlay's affections. She must be yearning for the sweet offer he dangled – the promise to come and join them for a holiday. He suggests Basel; she eagerly wonders if he could come sooner and join them in Hamburg. Something to look forward to. But first, to business. As we turn along the ragged coastline, island after island, rocks folding into rocks, I return to the pages of *Letters from Norway* with a sense of foreboding.

Wollstonecraft detests Risør with a venom that's strong even by her standards. The seedy people, dark smoky houses and glowering cliffs – everything here causes her disgust. "To be born here was to be bastilled by nature!" And she doesn't stop there: "There is a shrewdness in the character of these people, depraved by a sordid love of money, which repels me." Yet more inadequate dental hygiene: "disgusting" teeth. And although the men stink, the women aren't bothered: "It is well that the women are not very delicate, or they would only love their husbands because they were their husbands." Hey Wollstonecraft, why not tell us how you really feel about Risør?

Will and I are to be hosted by Norway's only communist mayor: Knut Henning Thygesen. Despite everything she says about the place, the mayor of Risør is a Wollstonecraft enthusiast and has offered us a place to stay for a few days. But he's away on holiday. Will and I will be on our own among the looming cliffs, where the "tremendous bulwarks enclosed" her "on every side", so that Wollstonecraft feels she can scarcely breathe. My expectations are low.

What a surprise, then, to sail into a town so dazzling it's as though it's been scrubbed with salty water and dried in the bleaching sun. It's early evening, and the late sun is dipping low. The houses are wooden, of course, and perfectly white. It's so white my eyes ache. I gratefully touch Anjava on my way back onto dry land. With sadness, Will and I fondly say goodbye to Mick and Gunnar, our captain and our shipmate.

Knut Henning Thygesen's house is up high, right on top of the cliffs that Wollstonecraft found so oppressive. It's next to the Risørflekken, a bungalow-sized white chalk circle marked onto the rocks. This is visible for miles out to sea and is used as a navigational landmark. Our new Norwegian home is a tiny studio flat at the bottom of Knut's tumbling garden. A cherry tree sweeps over it. Waist-high flowers, spilling yellow daises and bursting lilies lean into Will's buggy as we push through on the stone path.

I get Will ready for bed. We share my last squashed sandwich and before long we are both completely unconscious. To quote the great woman: "I sunk into the most luxurious rest; it was more than refreshing". Waking up in a new, unknown place is something wonderful. And if that new place is surrounded by flowers, has sunlight and birdsong streaming in and a view down to a blue sea, then you can feel pretty pleased with yourself. I open the fridge and find breakfast for Will and me: blueberry jam, soft brown bread and cheese.

To add to the profound joy, these wonderful strangers left not only a cot for Will but also a large plastic caterpillar, with flashing lights and big buttons that sing. Not the sort of thing I'd ever buy, let alone bring on a trip – but what, it turns out, do I know? The caterpillar is a piece of magnificent fortune. Will is entranced by it for at least forty minutes. During which time I have a slow shower, make a second coffee, and then sit blankly on a chair doing nothing at all. I haven't done this for ages.

It's pretty amazing.

Eventually we head down into town. It's steep. Will, the buggy and I gather momentum as we zip down to sea level. Bright boats are moored in the clean harbour, their masts jangling and clanging in the wind. Modest yet stylish shops sell linen clothing and white wicker baskets. It's a White Company catalogue come to life. The people are good-looking. The sea is bluer than a '70s postcard. Has the entire place been Photoshopped? It's almost too much. Can a place be this tidy, this stylish and still have humans in it? I put on my sunglasses. Only at the far end of the harbour do I spot a small dog poo near a bush, and a shopping trolley in the sea. I try not to smirk.

But what of the dark smoky houses, looming shadows and depraved, filthy people? Why does Wollstonecraft see so much ugliness here? I'm beginning to feel faintly disloyal for loving Risør when it was the scene of such misery for her. These cliffs don't torment my soul in the least. I fail to meet any scheming brown-toothed inhabitants. I do my best, but it's very hard to be unhappy here.

On top of it all, the people of Risør don't even seem to hold a grudge about Wollstonecraft's harsh words. I meet up with two of them: a retired history teacher, Kjell Arthur Paulsen, and the town's watchman, John Thomas Axelsen. Kjell Arthur has swept-back historian hair and impressive gravestone teeth. He has given lectures about Wollstonecraft's writing on the region. John Thomas, in his scarlet watchman's outfit with brass buttons, has a red leering face and a Sid James chuckle. "I was born in Risør and I thank almighty God for it," he announces.

"Right… but the place isn't quite how I expected it, as you can imagine," I begin.

"Ah, but do you know about the fire?" Kjell Arthur asks. "On the night of 6th June 1861 was the biggest fire in Risør's history. All our houses are made of wood – this is why we have a watchman, to go around at night looking out for fires. But 248 houses burned down that night. The men were out at sea. The women of Risør saved the church: they stood in a row passing buckets of water, while their own houses burned down. The church was built in 1647: it's the same one that Wollstonecraft mentions, and you still see it there today. Then town planning was changed, with wider streets to prevent fires, and this changed the whole aspect of Risør. This was the end of those dark alleys."

I describe the regularity of a terrace of English houses, and remark on the striking individuality of Norwegian houses. Kjell Arthur replies: "Yes! That is the Norwegian character. Wollstonecraft says that we are one of the freest, most liberated people in the world. We are separate from Europe, and we like being separate. When Britain was great, then they were separate too. Then they lost their status, and that's when they wanted to connect to Europe."

John Thomas chuckles again, and I smile to show that I'm totally OK with coming from a low-status country. Then I ask about the silver.

Kjell Arthur continues with increasing emphasis: "Mary *knew* that Ellefsen had the silver. It was she who wrote him the receipt. She was *there* when he took it on board. Ellefsen's mother was very rich, she owned the Egeland Ironworks. But even so, I think that it was Ellefsen who took it – it didn't disappear at the bottom of the sea, as some believe."

John Thomas leans forward and croaks "Lots of people dived for it. I knew a man called Charlie – he searched the islands here in the area for more than forty years. He came here from America, read all the history and spent forty years on diving expeditions, seeking that silver. He's dead now. But every week I teased him: "Have you found the silver yet?" – and he'd say: "No, not yet." He kept seeking it until his death."

"I love this kind of optimism," I say. "Doesn't part of you wish the silver was still out there somewhere, just glinting there, waiting to be hunted and discovered?"

"Well, a lot of people still sit watching at the side of Loch Ness too!" says Kjell Arthur, and they have a little guffaw together. Then, with an air of preventing further such nonsense, he continues:

"Wollstonecraft was well known. When she came on her travels, she was hailed because of her writing. She was well known in Paris too. And she was so sturdy." He swipes and pounds the table with his hands: "She had ideas about freedom and virtue. Virtue was at that time thought to be something that only men had – but this is nonsense, and I believe that this is why she almost killed herself twice, because she knew what this was all about. She's amazing for her time. She brought the discussion: what about the rights of woman, but also the rights of man – by this she means human rights."

John Thomas interrupts: "But she fell in *love* during the Revolution – she was in love with a man, and she forgot all about the rights of man and the Revolution." He's somewhat jeering now. "She left it all behind – for a *man*!" It's becoming clear that this particular citizen of Risør may not be quite as forgiving as the others.

"Actually, John Thomas," I smile at him, steely, full beam, "she wrote a book about the Revolution during this time. As well as becoming a mother. The fascination of her life is that there's so much to interpret. So people impose their own ideas and bring their own problems to her story."

As I hold forth it doesn't occur to me that this is what I'm doing too. But John Thomas is not the only critic to hold Wollstonecraft's passions against her – as though the act of falling in love deletes all her political arguments. And what's so wrong with love? If she'd never been in it, they'd all say what a dry old man-hater she was.

Kjell Arthur backs me up: "I'm very impressed by her, and I used to teach my students about half of the world's population and their lack of rights for the last several thousand years." Kjell Arthur has an eagerness, almost an impatience, when speaking that must have made him an outstanding teacher. "When I read about Mary I was impressed by what she did."

I notice that he calls her Mary and wonder why I have always called her Wollstonecraft. A sneaking envy creeps into me, even though it would be weird to change now, at the idea of this casual intimacy. I swallow the feeling, because at least he's a co-fanatic, and there aren't nearly enough of us after all. Changing the subject, I mention the encounter with the historian back in Kragerø. The one who said: bah, that feminist, she's all about the emotions.

"We-e-ll," says Kjell Arthur, "in her meetings with people when she was angry – perhaps you could have said to her: calm down. Talk quietly when you meet Ellefsen. Calm down and talk to him quietly, and then perhaps you will reach your goal. But she was fierce. She was filled with all the injustices facing women: she saw this in France, she saw it in her girls' school in England, she saw it in her father, a drunk man behaving badly towards her mother, and all of this collected up. She saw so much, and she understood, and that's why she behaved like this."

"Calm down and talk quietly" sounds rather a Norwegian piece of relationship advice. Not quite Wollstonecraft's style, though. What if the whole thing was a fool's errand? Was Imlay deploying her but hiding all the facts? Or simply trying to distract her after the suicide attempt? Kjell Arthur insists not:

"No. She understood. She is too intelligent not to know why he pushed her away: she knew why he pushed her away, but she said OK, this trip might be good for me, I want to do this, and then perhaps I will win him back. And of course she was in love too."

"Yes," I get animated, "she was in love and also a believer in people's ability to change, in the perfectibility of mankind – so she must have thought that he would change."

"Ha – every woman wants to change a man!" shouts John Thomas. "It's the same old story! We all know it!" And even Will joins in the cackling as hilarity breaks out all round.

Chapter Six

Obvious Progress

The next morning we make a discovery, Will and I. Behind Knut's house, past a laburnum tree in yellow bloom, full of bumble bees, is a small pathway leading into some woods. We wander in, in the early sunlight. There are trees, both evergreen and deciduous, all around. Thick mosses cover the ground. Moving further into the woods is a lake. It is in fact the perfect lake. It's hidden, quiet and clear, and there's a wooden diving board sticking off the end of a huge rock. I have a surge of missing Justin and the girls – they would run completely wild here.

The winding path continues beyond the lake, coming out abruptly onto a viewing point high in the air above a wealth of scattered islands. It's sheltered from the wind, and sunny. This is my new favourite place, my equivalent of Wollstonecraft's Tønsberg hilltop. The air catches the sounds of boats from far below and lifts them up to me. I look down on the backs of birds swooping out from the cliffs below. There are bushes covered in tiny roses, and the smell mingles with the pine.

I take some photos, try to record the sound of a bumble bee, and wish I could store the smell of the air. I sit down and take out the book to read out loud:

What, indeed, is to humanize these beings, who rest shut up, for they seldom even open their windows, smoking, drinking brandy and driving bargains? I have been almost stifled by these smokers. They begin in the morning, and are rarely without their pipe till they go to bed. Nothing can be more disgusting than the rooms and men towards the evening: breath, teeth, clothes and furniture all are spoilt...

But reading on a bit, she doesn't hate for too long. Quite the opposite. Even here she sees people's future potential. Even in hated Risør, she sees

the first steps of the improvement which I am persuaded will make a very obvious progress in the course of half a century; and it ought not to be sooner, to keep pace with the cultivation of the earth. Improving manners will introduce finer moral feelings.

Fifty years? She reckons the human race only needs another fifty years to mature morally, to pull up its collective socks and become worthy of her love. Fifty years of cultivation. Humanity as an orchard or wheat field. So we should have had it all sorted by 1845? I imagine showing her the world of today. Would she capsize us all in a towering storm of indignation? Or would her "ardent affection" persist? I believe that it would. And that it doesn't matter if she's wrong to believe in human perfectibility. She is also right to believe in it.

My vague desire was that something would rub off on me on this journey – that I too would undergo some of her "cultivation". But everything is so smooth and contented – how can this lead to "improvement" and "progress"? Some churning discovery was supposed to emerge from her words, a kick in the shin directly from 1795 to this moment, alerting me to... something. Maybe even delivering up a few of those "finer moral feelings". But instead she's suffering away like she bloody well invented it, and I'm smelling the flowers. Does this make me one of those inward-looking "smokers" who never opens the window?

A jogging woman suddenly pops out of the bushes and runs past, turning her head in a laughing greeting as she goes. I laugh too, and gather up my stuff. The shin kick will come when it's ready. As we walk back into the gentle pine-smelling woods, a crowd of blue tits rushes by, ruffling the air.

Will is asleep, lying in an oddly polite way, his legs tucked in, his hands folded. I lean in as close as possible, watch his chest rise and fall, look at the small dimples on the backs of his hands. I lightly trace the back of his hand with my finger. Without waking him, I want him to know that this is one of the best days of my life and he's in it too.

When Knut, in whose garden we're so genteelly residing, comes back to town, he invites me round for a plate of mackerels in yogurt and a bowl of fresh salty prawns. Will gobbles these as quickly as I can peel off their extremities. Surely the Mayor of Risør shouldn't be allowed to like Wollstonecraft, after all she said? Knut laughs. "For about ten years I was indignant, then I discovered much more about her, and now I'm glad – I'm proud that she was here." We discuss her excitedly, like proper Wollstonecraft geeks. Our mackerels in yogurt go cold in the slanting evening sun.

If you could choose a family to be an advert for Norway, it would be Knut's family. They are outdoorsy, they tease each other, they eat freshly baked bread together for breakfast. And they are so impossibly attractive that you get embarrassed looking at them. Knut has wild bushy hair and leaves his shirt open. His wife, Tina Bang, has high cheekbones, large eyes and the best name ever. Their son Espen is handsome, studious and interested in the world. There are also two beautiful daughters whose photos adorn the walls. Like their hometown, they are a vision of wholesomeness. They have, after all, invited a complete stranger and her baby to live in their garden while they were away on holiday.

Will and I join them for breakfast, coming up the stony path from our garden home. All of the food in the house is placed onto a groaning wooden table. Within my immediate reach I find eggs, several cheeses, fish, meat, butter, bread, jams, berries, juice, coffee and some strange things in jars. They might be baby octopuses. "So you're writing a book? What's it about?" says Tina Bang. "It's about travelling with a baby," I say, as Will thrashes in my arms by way of asking to be put on the floor. She smiles fondly as he crawls away towards some tomato plants.

I want to know more about how Wollstonecraft's reaction to Risør might have been influenced by the events in her life at the time. "She was here looking for Ellefsen," says Knut. "But the most interesting thing is how the psychological effects come out, how this determines what you will write. She was extremely disappointed here. I think that explains what she wrote. If you read the Bible or history from thousands of years ago, people are writing their own subjective version."

"I think so too," I join in, "but that's just my subjective version of her subjective version."

"But, you know, Risør could have been a bad place," adds Tina, the first person to voice this possibility. "And maybe the people weren't so nice. Strange things happen here in Risør. It was a rich town, but the people were getting rich in a bad way: there were smugglers and a lot of monkey business. My family has been here in Risør since 1780; my ancestor had a brandy distillery."

I recall Wollstonecraft describing the smelly people of Risør pushing the brandy bottle around all day. Espen interrupts: "They still do. That was probably our great-great-great-great-great-grandfather pushing that bottle of brandy."

"People drank a lot," Tina adds. "It's a harbour, of course – because of this, I think it's true what she wrote; I think it was not too nice when she was here. Every tree was chopped down back then. For fuel and shipbuilding. It wasn't good: no green, and a lot of people drinking."

"If a place like Risør used to be like that, then there's hope for us all," I say. "How else has it changed, compared to back then?" "Today it's much more equal," says Knut. "But Risør still has problems, especially in the summer. You see it when the rich people come from Oslo. The local people are happy to have guests, but we are afraid that they will buy up holiday homes. There is a law about second homes, but people know how to get round this: they give it to their children, and still keep the place empty, while the local people cannot buy. We want to protect houses by making people live here all year round if they buy a place."

"Is it true that you're a communist?" I ask.

"No he's not!" says Tina.

"Let *him* answer!"

Knut laughs: "She decides, of course! No, really – I'm not like a Soviet Communist – that was a horrible civilization I think. But I dream about a society where all people are equal. The right wing is gaining influence here: they talk of freedom, of individual politics. But this isn't about freedom: it's only freedom for the few. A hundred years ago we were one of the poorest countries in Europe, and then we found the oil, and today we are the richest. But when a country becomes rich so quickly—"

He's interrupted by some gargling noises coming from Will. Perched in his baby chair, he's stuffed too much bread into his mouth. We jump up and fuss over him. He emits a stream of sodden chunks and then smiles. I mention the young Swedish couple who gave him sweets on the bus, and how surprising it was that they were economic migrants. There is unmistakable glee at this. Tina says: "They always looked down on us, the Danish and the Swedish. In particular the Swedish. When I was young, I went Inter-railing, and in Sweden they'd say: 'Ha ha, you are Norwegian, you smell of fish.'"

There's a pause. "Perhaps you did," says Knut.

They laugh. Tina turns and sings a song to Will. He laughs; she chuckles and squeaks at him; he claps his hands. He does his unhinged smile, so big that you can see every one of his teeth. Everyone stops to watch him, and I'm suddenly bathed in motherly pride. He is so eye-achingly perfect that I have to feign some modesty. I roll my eyes and tell him off: "What are you doing, fiendish tyke?" But secretly I want to burst with love.

"But there's another side," Knut tries again "when you get rich in a hurry, that influences your thinking as a nation—"

Will heaves the coffee jug over into a basket of bread, from where the hot black flood spreads into Tina's lap. My smugness evaporates as Tina leaps up to get changed and we dab at the coffee with tea towels. I realize very much later that we never did find out what happens to nations that get rich in a hurry. Norway is indeed the happy owner of a whopping oil fortune, but by the time we've stemmed the coffee tide, we're back onto Wollstonecraft's journey again, and an even more unrecognized heroine.

"Wollstonecraft travelled by ship at this time, as a woman with a baby, on the North Sea, because she wanted to prove something: women could do anything men could do. And she also had a tough maid. Here is a question. Where is the history of the maid? She is just as impressive, perhaps. The maid had a tough time." Knut pauses. "You see, there is the history of the known people, but what about the history of the people who are keeping the known people getting known? Marguerite is this person."

Hours later, still recovering from the epic breakfast, I think about Marguerite and those unknown people who keep the known people known. Was Wollstonecraft good to Marguerite? She defends vulnerable women, but does this play out in her treatment of her and Frances's faithful companion?

Marguerite's appearances in *Letters from Norway* are fleeting – there's not that much of an impression. Which is odd, because Wollstonecraft goes off all the time about how Swedish women treat their servants.

Marguerite started working for Wollstonecraft back in Paris. She gets debilitating seasickness every time they travel in a boat. She is scared of steep roads and cautious of strangers. "Poor Marguerite!" says Wollstonecraft breezily (she never gets seasick and is never cautious). Marguerite is also a first-hand witness to Wollstonecraft's agonies with Imlay. It is she who is sent, again and again and again, to strange post offices in the hope of collecting a letter from him. There must have been many occasions to think, *"Mon Dieu*, I didn't sign up for this."

Towards the end, when they're homeward-bound, Wollstonecraft, Frances and Marguerite are travelling from Denmark to Germany. They've been on the road for some time. When Marguerite and baby Frances both fall asleep, Wollstonecraft is relieved – they have so little in common. Marguerite's excitable chattering about the strange foreign fashions begins to grate. But she poignantly adds that Marguerite's "happy thoughtlessness" and *"gaité du cœur"* are "worth all my philosophy". If only she, like Marguerite, could simply be happy...

Even if Wollstonecraft sounds high-handed, it's unlikely that she was unkind to her chirpy companion. At least, I don't want her to be, so I plough around for evidence. Her *Original Stories*, an early kids' book of excruciating primness, has a worthy chapter on 'Behaviour to Servants – True Dignity of Character'. And although Wollstonecraft certainly gave her peers the haranguing of their lives, her future husband Godwin writes: "To her servants there was never a mistress more considerate or kind."

She herself describes with the usual indignation how

...ladies of the most exquisite sensibility, who were continually exclaiming against the cruelty of the vulgar to the brute creation, have in my presence forgot that their attendants had human feelings, as well as forms. I do not know of a more agreeable sight than to see servants part of a family.

But what Wollstonecraft doesn't do is reflect on her own privilege in the current scenario: the fact that she is being enabled in her quest, as Knut points out, by another woman's hard work. And what irony that, until now, neither do I. Searching back and forth for Marguerite references in Wollstonecraft's book while capering around on a fabulous adventure. And far away back home, my own nanny, Nori, steps up whenever Justin's sent on another foreign trip.

Remember how I resented Wollstonecraft that early morning in Kragerø – oh well, it's fine for her, she's got a maid – remember that? It's also true of me, and why it's possible for me to do this. If it wasn't for Nori... The thought trails out and leaves me uncomfortable. We've all heard the breezy career mum describing her nanny as "like my wife!" This complex relationship between women, of co-dependency and hierarchy, is an untapped source.

Elephant taps on door: hello, just popping round to come and sit in the middle of your room. Middle-class women are the direct beneficiaries of this inequality: it's a source of both freedom and guilt. So far I have avoided looking the elephant in the eye. Something tells me this may not last much longer.

Wollstonecraft has done both sides. She was once a governess. She's almost certainly suffering from depression, and it's not her finest hour. The letters she sends to her sisters reveal something of a nightmare employee, and at least three of Wollstonecraft's biographers feel sympathy with her boss, Lady Kingsborough. In episodes that have a flavour of modern kiss-and-tell, Wollstonecraft spills the nanny beans on the lisping, decadent mother who prefers to lie around in satins with her lap dogs rather than care for her children.

When Lady K tries to include her governess socially at fancy parties, Wollstonecraft sees the invitations as patronizing and enraging, and uses them to satirize her boss. (Despite her vast wealth, Lady Kingsborough was married off aged fifteen for "breeding". She bore twelve children and had no significant education. Maybe, just maybe, her rights needed vindicating too?) The lady tries to give the governess a cheap cotton dress. Wollstonecraft not only rejects it, but storms off and sulks in her room until Lady K has to come and apologize to her.

Wollstonecraft boasts that the children like her more than their mother. Even if this is true, she relishes it too much: "At the sight of their mother they tremble and run to me for protection" and the "sweet little boy ... calls himself my son". And while sulking in her room, Wollstonecraft is also writing a book, *Mary: A Fiction*, in which the eponymous heroine's rouge-cheeked mother packs her children off to be cared for by nurses, while she lies on cushions playing with her dogs. Beware the revenge of the nanny.

There's something unsettling in the stand-off between a chippy young Wollstonecraft and her aristocratic new environment. Wollstonecraft picks incessantly on Lady K's looks and beauty regime, but his Lordship rarely takes any flack. Surely he gave as much cause for anger? But he gets off lightly. It's the yawnsome old spectacle of the catfight. It's easier to slag women off for having childcare than to address the bigger picture. I've done it myself. My heart sinks a little that Wollstonecraft did it too.

If anything, Wollstonecraft's own governess memories should make her more supportive of the loyal and cheerful Marguerite. I think again about my nanny, Nori. Like Marguerite, she is impressive. She finished her degree in a second language alongside working with us. She works part-time, and if it's been a few days since her last shift I physically droop with relief when she walks in the door. She's seen us through house moves, nit infestations, miscarriages, pregnancy and newborn madness. She puts up with chaos, shouty arguments and unpredictability; in exchange she provides stability and calm. In short, she delivers sanity. How do you thank someone for that?

Gratitude doesn't come easily where childcare is involved. I'd like to blame this thought on someone else, but secretly I've thought it myself: childcare should be good and lovable, but not *too* good and lovable. Do mothers resent success in a carer? Of course! It's hard enough to love your own kids all day long. How much harder must it be if they're someone else's, poking your bum and asking about muffin tops? I think for a while about how to be more appreciative. Then sigh with satisfaction about my benevolent intentions. It's easy to be a good person at long distance.

The sunlight here intensifies in the late afternoon. It'll be light for many more hours, but this light is special. The sea, the sky and even the shadows are a brilliant demented blue. We wander along the harbour to the Risør Fiskemottak, where fishing boats unload their catch. Will discovers Norwegian fishcakes, wiping them in his hair to the delight of the people at the next table, and I drink black coffee.

What is the magic of being near water? Risør sits in a natural harbour facing a sprinkle of skerries: small uninhabited rocky islands, where families in boats potter around, fishing and paddling. The lure of these tiny islands is strong: there is magic in the notion of a miniature world, of setting foot on a child-sized kingdom. Watery adventures from childhood books spring to mind: *The Wind in the Willows* and *Swallows and Amazons*. I long and long for my other kids. Being in kid-heaven makes their absence sharper.

I didn't expect to find so much happiness in Wollstonecraft's erratic footsteps, and I'm grateful that they brought us to Risør. I will never forget being in this place, with scattering blue light and baby Will attacking the fishcakes. I'm plagued, however, by how dramatically our reactions have diverged. Wollstonecraft came here and everything went wrong. From Risør it only gets darker and bleaker. She starts quoting Hamlet – never a good sign. Even the usually beloved pine trees make her want to die:

The pine and fir woods, left entirely to nature, display an endless variety; and the paths in the wood are not entangled with fallen leaves, which are only interesting whilst they are fluttering between life and death. The grey cobweb-like appearance of the aged pines is a much finer image of decay; the fibres whitening as they lose their moisture, imprisoned life seems to be stealing away. I cannot tell why – but death, under every form, appears to me like something getting free – to expand in I know not what element; nay, I feel that this conscious being must be as unfettered, have the wings of thought, before it can be happy.

Wollstonecraft has hit a new low. The mission has collapsed scarcely halfway through the book. She's left Risør and is heading back to collect her much-missed baby, to travel onwards with her and Marguerite. They still have Denmark and Germany to get through. There are repeated references to death and suicide, and I'm afraid for her. She has failed.

To find out how she failed I need to see Gunnar Molden again. Because there's no one alive who knows more about this part of the journey. He has invited me to come and see his archives, in the town of Arendal. Arendal is further west than Wollstonecraft came, and was the family home of Captain Peder Ellefsen.

Gunnar's office is inside Arendal's original town hall. Despite all our high jinx and cinnamon buns on the ocean wave, Gunnar is still shy. He tenses up when I switch on my recording equipment. At first his answers are halting and short. I ask how long he's been working on Wollstonecraft. "Only part-time, in my spare time. I started twenty years ago. It all began with *Letters from Norway*, the Richard Holmes edition—"

"Me too," I shout, the enthusiast overcoming the journalist in me. He pauses politely. I apologize and indicate silently for him to go on.

"The main story is of course what happened to the silver. We still haven't found it. It's very probable that Peder Ellefsen stole the silver, but he was not alone: he had some associates, and it's possible that they forced him. When Wollstonecraft met him in Risør, she tried to get an out-of-court settlement. It is possible that he wanted to do it, but couldn't because of their influence on him. Publicly he denied having ever received any silver. And Wollstonecraft couldn't prove it. Ellefsen just completely denied it, which ended up being a successful defence."

Some of the details of Wollstonecraft's battle have only emerged in recent years. She went right to the top, roping in the Prime Minister of Denmark, then the ruling colonial power in Norway. And it was Gunnar, researching in his own time, living far away from national archives, who threw light on this. I ask Gunnar about his 2003 discovery of the Wollstonecraft letter, and he laughs nervously:

"It's one of the finest experiences I've had. I was in Copenhagen and I'd spent nearly a week going through documents. I saw all kinds of other information about the case. I only had one week and I was running out of time. I found a file in a box marked *Madame Imlay's Case*." He pauses. "It was then that I understood I'd found one of the most important things."

He avoids eye contact. I pry further: "Come on, what did it *feel* like?"

He lets out a giggle, "It felt… almost like proof that God exists!" He pauses again, an even longer pause, then heaves down several more boxes, rummages in them and passes me some large sheets of paper. I'm holding the photocopied pages of Mary Wollstonecraft's letter. Here she is. I get a surge of affection seeing her determined, slightly loopy handwriting.

"It's in perfect condition," Gunnar says quietly. We look at the pages. I get a churchy kind of feeling and scarcely dare breathe on them.

"Her handwriting is not modern, but I'm used to reading Gothic script, and these are Latin letters, so it's not hard to read. Of course I feel closer to her as a person, reading this. It's important as found information – as a historian it's important. But on a personal level it's… it's…"

I nod and smile, willing him on.

"…it's… Well. I really enjoyed it."

This is as effusive as he's going to get. But instead of wishing I could get a better soundbite out of him, I'm struck with admiration. I'd mistaken his quietness for an absence, a lack of something: I was wrong. Gunnar spent his free time searching through years of false starts, misspellings and boxes of old paper, and he didn't do it for glory. His thoughtfulness and precision make me feel cartoony and frivolous in comparison. Certain qualities are likely to advance humanity, such as curiosity and perseverance. And this man has them in spades.

The letter itself is a summary of the case against Ellefsen, and a plea for the Prime Minister to intervene on her behalf. The original is now in the Rigsarkivet, the National Archives of Denmark. Gunnar tells how she describes the meeting with

Ellefsen in Risør, how he is "humble" and regretful. She persuades him to bring compensation from his wealthy family. He returns later the same day, but in a very different mood. He's spoken to his lawyers and is suddenly all a-swagger. Whatever advice he's been given, it's clear that she will now get neither compensation nor silver.

Will feels the need to put in an appearance at this stage. He rapidly builds up to a thrashing wail in his buggy, and to cheer him up we head out for a wander around Arendal. We stop in the Strand Kafé, Gunnar's favourite, and I find a baby chair for Will. We order a *monke*, a small sweet dumpling, and some black coffee. Will drinks his milk thoughtfully, and I pass him little pieces of *monke* to chew.

Leaving the café, we climb up the hill and sit on a bench, overlooking some old cannons facing out to sea. At last I bring up the relationship between him and Wollstonecraft. The one that had seemed so unlikely when we first met. Why her, of all the women in all the books in all the world? Why does Wollstonecraft walk into Gunnar's gin joint?

He breaks into a smile.

"I've always been interested in the connections between my local region and the world, and this is a perfect example. Personally, Wollstonecraft's text makes it so easy to engage with her, she's very subjective – and I like that. *Ja*. Why? Well. Maybe I'm a romantic person myself…"

But then we're drawn back again, into the misery. It's no longer just Ellefsen and the missing silver, there's another massive body blow to come. All this time Wollstonecraft has been expecting a reunion with Imlay – their romantic holiday together. But he's gone cold. He is gradually withdrawing from his promise to join her. And so her letters become more bitter: she guilt-trips him about their baby, once more she's struggling to keep going.

I tell Gunnar that I find some of the post-Risør letters difficult to read. There's a growing sense of disgust, of pointlessness. A "black melancholy hovers round my footsteps", she writes, describing "a sensibility wounded almost to madness". It's eating away at her. Yet on she goes, carrying onwards to Copenhagen and Hamburg and whatever secret unfinished business it is that Imlay's putting her up to.

Here Gunnar has even more fuel for despair. He has his own theory about what that business might be:

"Imlay was a small player, but with important and influential contacts. I'm speculating here, but it's possible that she has discovered that he's dealing arms to France. Another possibility is gunpowder. Imlay's plan was to use the silver to buy 'provisions' to bring back to France. The question is: were these provisions food or weapons? There's a big difference. And the British said you weren't even allowed to let food in – that was the blockade against France."

Weapons-dealing! Such goings-on might explain the references to "vile trade" and "mushroom fortunes". Also why she goes back from Scandinavia via Hamburg; the business centre for these important contacts of Imlay's. Wollstonecraft's penultimate letter seems to support Gunnar's theory. "These men," she writes, with energetic fury, "like the owners of negro ships, never smell on their money the blood by which it has been gained." In the middle of one of her diatribes against "sordid accumulators" she suddenly zooms in:

But you will say that I am growing bitter, perhaps personal. Ah! Shall I whisper to you that you yourself are strangely altered since you have entered deeply into commerce?

Is Wollstonecraft complicit? No one knows how much she knew. But you can bet she knew enough. Such business would be a betrayal, would compromise her completely. In Gunnar's discovered letter, where Wollstonecraft pleads her case to the Prime Minister, she proudly invokes her character as "a moral writer". Has she put her credibility at stake, and compromised her beliefs for Imlay? While he's just gone and dumped her again? I chase away a small dog that's come over and is sniffing Will's leg. All three of us stare silently over the grey water for a while.

"What about France?" I ask. "She still wants to return and live there, but some of the violence has a profound effect on her. Do you think Wollstonecraft fell out of love with the Revolution after what she witnessed? Doesn't she call Robespierre a monster?"

"Yes, she fell out of love with the bloody part of it. She basically kept the same opinion about all things, but was disappointed by what she saw, and when she came here to Norway she was shocked by people supporting Robespierre. She had the first-hand experience that they did not. The people who began the Revolution, they had no idea how it would go. It's part of the human experience to watch how it goes without knowing. Look what's happening in Arab countries now."

"Another reason we should learn from Wollstonecraft today."

"Yes. That sense of uncertainty: we think it's a good thing, but we're not sure. This is the ideal moment to reflect on her times, as we're in huge shifting times now ourselves. But Revolutions like this become very doubtful when they start using weapons."

"But you can't just ask a dictator to step aside, can you?" I say.

"No, but you should wait as long as possible."

"That's all very polite, but if you were Syrian right now you might be arming to protect your kids. And don't you think Syrians have waited? They've waited and waited and waited…"

"Ok, it's inhuman to expect them to wait for ever," Gunnar replies, "but I think the results are better without violence. I hope for change in Iraq, Afghanistan, but of course we have to be lucky."

"Do you believe in luck?

"I don't know."

"How about God?"

"I don't know. I hope there's a God." He laughs. "This goes on the list of things I need to prove."

The wind blows a paper bag onto Will's buggy wheels. A seagull swoops, then lands nearby and looks at us sideways. We look out to sea.

Chapter Seven

"To Achieve That Moral Improvement within Half a Century"

The correct antidote to dusty boxes full of despair is to go out on a boat. We meet up with some of Gunnar's family and friends, and all head out for a picnic on the island of Merdø. Lucky I'm not French, I snigger. Gunnar's daughter Jenny joins us; she's ten and reminds me of my daughters. We sit together and I resist the urge to hug her in an act of surrogacy – I miss my girls so. The picnic includes fishcakes. Will and I set to, and I keep him on my lap as a pretext for eating a few more, while Jenny practises her English on me. Afterwards, as we step back into the boat to set off, Gunnar turns to me with a quiet smile.

"There's one more place to show you."

We moor up on a jetty belonging to an elegant house in Sandviga. A dashing man is standing there waiting, with tweeds and slicked-back hair like a matinée idol. He is called Terje Bodin Larsen, and he has a very large handshake. This is his house, and it's the last known place that the silver was ever seen.

"They unloaded the silver from the ship *right here*." Gunnar points out an iron hook sunk deep into the rock, to which they would have moored. "After that, nobody knows."

Terje tells me that a survey was done along the coast in 1738 placing these mooring arrangements by issue of decree. The hook has been there ever since, he adds, "but I still haven't seen any silver!"

After that, nobody knows.

Then the silver trail stops here. This is as far as we can go. A yellow sun streams all around us. It's that mad hour of sunlight – it beams down into the water, shining clear right down to the bottom. There's a diving board sticking off the jetty over the bright water. It's salt water, but it looks as clear as the purest river. It's the same buttery light that welcomed us when we first arrived in Norway, and it makes me feel drunk. It's the same exhilaration I could barely contain on board Anjava. The same purity that dazzled me in Risør.

This place and moment are of such significance, they deserve some kind of ritual. A solemn dedication. I look around for an accomplice, and there's one right here. Gunnar's daughter is playing with my phone. "Jenny, do you want to jump in with me?" "Yes!" A girl of action, like my daughters. I pause for a second – Will is being adored by people while working his way through a bowl of gleaming strawberries – then strip to my T shirt and knickers. Laughing, Jenny and I hold hands and leap off the jetty diving board together.

Cold water closes over us as we plunge deep. Time freezes for a split second as I look up into the swirl of bubbles, trapped laughter, silver air, rising above my head. This is it! I say to myself, not knowing what it means, then we burst back up, panting. We immediately do it again to make sure it was real, limbs scrambling in the chilly water. One last breathless go

– I can't resist. And then I creep into Terje's house to dress, stuffing my soggy things into my jacket pockets. My breath, my skin, the hairs on my skin – everything's heightened. I go commando, and feel invincible.

Terje hands out wine in heavy goblets, the sun streams through the liquid. The wine hits me right there. At the same euphoric instant, absurdly, a small orchestra warms up and begins to play, sitting outdoors just two jetties away. It's altogether too much. Violins – you must be kidding. In a climactic finale, this sensory overload collides with my private mixed-up feelings of an ending; the trail's ending. Like the rainbow trailing into the pot of gold. The music floats over to us like a spell, the golden sun is in my eyes, and the silver trail ends.

What treasures have I gathered? My mind greedily amasses a wealth that I can roll in and let cascade through my fingers. I've gathered up times of joy and adventure with Will to save – to store life-long. The water, the bubbles of light in the water, sunbeams, strawberries, the music. Me and the boy, already I can see us as if from afar. I've collected a luminous string of people who have welcomed and helped us. And I've trodden in her footsteps, walked and sailed and scrambled right behind her, and read her words aloud.

As Wollstonecraft's journey gets darker, mine keeps on gathering light.

She was so brave. I knew she was brave before, but I hadn't seen those spiky rocks jutting up out of the sea, and hadn't launched myself among far-off strangers with my baby. I feel disloyal at what a relief it is, getting out from between her darkening words for the last few days of our Norway trip. Sometimes I think I'm just too happy to hang around with Wollstonecraft. She'd think I was a bit of a lightweight, no doubt. In the couple of days we have left, Will and I meander slowly and easily to Oslo.

As we leave Wollstonecraft's trail behind us, there's more time to think about Norway, and how it's my new favourite place. This is a country that includes and celebrates children by design. I've seen a strange contraption that turned out to be a pram on skis, allowing babies to join in the snowy winter action. I've seen street signs showing that a child playing football has priority over a car. And in a strange twist Norwegian children, the wealthiest in Europe, have a closeness to nature and wilderness that's more often the preserve of impoverished children. It's not uncommon to see a seven-year-old child fishing or managing a small boat with an outboard motor on her own.

Wilderness is precious, and Norwegians value it. Space is common. Garden fences are rare. They have a cherished law: *allemannsret* – the right of everyone to roam freely in Norway's open spaces, as long as nothing is disturbed. Not to mention the equality, the Peace Prize and all that. Wollstonecraft praised Norway back then; nowadays I reckon she'd queue up for citizenship. Will and I have felt safe and welcome, everywhere. Of course, we've spent the whole time in rural Norway, in the summer. It can't all be wild cloudberries and fairy-looking children. There must be a dark side. What about that famous alcoholism, the winters, those violent crime thrillers?

Will and I stop over in Oslo. The city is obviously more edgy than where we've been, but there's still no sign of a shocking underbelly. It's increasingly clear that the Norwegians have it all worked out, that civilization thing. Wollstonecraft would not be disappointed by this city. Oslo seems to lack that desperate urban drift, the expanses of poverty that hover around cities like a smell that people learn to ignore. The rudest thing we've seen so far is still that shopping trolley in the sea back in Risør. And even that had been tidied away by the next day.

Behind the station is an immigrant market. I buy a samosa from a stall. The man is from Pakistan. He tells me in perfect English that he also speaks Norwegian. I go into a corner shop for water, and fall into conversation with the owner about Snus. Snus are extremely popular Scandinavian tobacco pouches. They look like a wrong teabag. You put them inside your cheek and they make your teeth go bright brown. "Here – take one," says the shop owner, proffering his own Snus stash. "It's healthier than smoking a cigarette." I try one. It's more villainous than burnt rubber. I attempt to thank him, and he laughs. Will and I trundle on through Oslo, looking round shops full of things we can't afford.

We end up at a Diversity Festival on a university campus. There's music by the Afro-Norwegian band Queendom, stalls promoting cultural tolerance and blonde kids running around dressed in turbans. Will and I tuck into some falafel. How adorable, I muse – but is it really necessary? It's so right-on, so advanced here in Norway: surely they must be post-diversity by now? I sigh irritably. Don't you simply live with diversity, and the point is that finally you stop even seeing it as such?

Will totters around in front of some drummers while I examine my private dissent from the celebrations. I can't yet tell if I'm just choking on the wholesomeness of it all, or if there's a proper argument for not celebrating diversity. This, after all, is why I live in London – I see different sorts of people every day, and that's just normal and how it should be. I don't feel the need to burst into song about it. "Festival of Diversity," I sneer, in my urban wisdom. "What's the point?"

The answer comes much sooner than I expect.

Three weeks later is the massacre. A Christian fundamentalist blows up eight people and then shoots a further sixty-nine people, mostly children. It's his way of showing that he doesn't want any more Muslims in his country. I'm back at home, frozen, unable to leave the house. I can't stop myself watching the story as it breaks. How could it happen here, of all places? Norwegians, my newly beloved friends, are all over the news in the shape of innocent children fleeing a lone gunman. He is armed with a rifle and a handgun, to which he has given names from Norse mythology. And he is carrying "dum-dum" bullets, designed for their expanding rounds. These cause greater internal tissue damage and leave a large exit wound.

Two hours earlier he had set off a car bomb in Oslo that killed eight people working in a government building. He intended to kill as many journalists as possible, but settled for government workers. He couldn't get the right parking spot either, and was upset about the angle at which he parked, because it diminished the impact. Another hitch was the delivery of his "manifesto" to other extremists. He's been getting this ready for a decade or so, but now that he tries to send it out, the repeating "error" messages of the Outlook mailing system cause a delay in his plans.

But once he heads north to the island of Utøya, his luck changes. Utøya is a holiday island owned by the ruling Labour Party's youth wing. They host summer camps here for bright young things who want to make the world better. The Norwegian police are miles away, concentrating on the Oslo attack, and their boats are out of order, and the helicopter team is on holiday. He can really take his time here.

The man is dressed as a police officer. News of the Oslo attack has reached the island and everyone's relieved to see a policeman. He calls the children to come and gather round, and they obey. He puts down his bag, and pulls out his guns, and he starts killing them. He strides along the beach as they scream and run away. Some beg for their lives, and are shot at close range. Some are paralysed with fear and just stand there, motionless. He kills them too. He pursues them methodically, firing round after round, and going back to make sure he hasn't missed. Those who have fallen and are injured are shot in the head. He shouts, "You will die today, Marxists!" He has brought drinking water, so as not to get a dry throat.

Children run into caves, toilets, behind rocks, bushes and trees. Some are given away when their mobile phones ring, and they are shot dead. In the canteen, some plead with him and are shot at point-blank range. He combs the woodland and beaches of the tiny island, ending young lives as he goes. Many try to escape into the water, struggling to swim to safety. One victim drowns, another dies fleeing off a cliff. The man goes about his work, undisturbed for around ninety minutes.

He aims at them, one by one, sometimes using the handgun and then the rifle too. He steadily reloads as they flail in the blue Norwegian water.

The collapsing feeling I get inside rips away at the light tissue of my golden trip. Closing my eyes, I can't stop seeing the children in the water and the corpses on the beach. I think about my Norwegian friends – their children and my children – and I cry. I see Wollstonecraft, dreaming of her daughter's tiny footsteps on the sand. Dreaming of a time, soon, when civilization would be complete. Perfectibility, she believed. We've got a long way to go.

Chapter Eight

Baby, You Can Drive My Career

How to write about motherhood? Step into the ever-expanding blogosphere and before you even get to "mommy wars" you'll find that mothering is nothing less than a human rights conflict, and as a mother you're on the front line. It starts with some pungent nappy talk: nappies leaking, nappies smelling and changing nappies every moment of the night and day. Screaming is the next key ingredient. Your baby screams like no baby has screamed before. Don't forget how knackered you look, how no one fancies you and even if they did you've lost your sex drive: you can actually see your own eye bags, and your breasts feel offended.

There should be sick on your T-shirt of course, and snot and milk on your remaining clothes. These clothes are stretchy and drab, and probably smelly. The buggy that you push around is like a ball and chain, a visual reminder of your enslaved status. Your hair should be a mess. Mums with good hair or make-up are bitches, trying to make the school run even worse than it already is.

A comedy moment is helpful, especially if it includes a useless dad. Useless Dad always forgets something vital, like milk or nappies, and then just goes back to work. So selfish. Another source of hilarity is how your once-sacred handbag now includes a dummy and some Calpol. Unbelievable. How about accidentally pulling out a baby-related item, under circumstances that will cause maximum awkwardness? Perhaps in front of people who have proper jobs and have never seen such a thing as a baby's toy before.

You might pause and think back to your own mum, and wonder how she did it. Or all the other mums throughout history and around the world. How do they manage? It's simple. They're not as tired or as busy as you. It all boils down to the injustice that no one told you it would be like this. So it's your duty to lift the lid on it. You may mutter, and we're going off-road now, that you don't even like your own baby. In fact you hate him and think he'll end up a psychopath. Sisters around the world will salute you for saying the unsayable. You may even get a film deal.

There's another unsayable: you're basically too clever for this. Sitting in a room full of mums singing 'Wind the Bobbin up'? Pushing a swing for an hour? That's OK for some people, but frankly, you used to have a PA/be creative/do proper things for actual money. There may be a class element here that you don't feel you have to explore too deeply, as there's no point wondering how poor people make it work. They probably get their mums to help or something.

Do not admit that there is smugness in the relief that you feel when you hear about someone's fertility struggles. Or that you can't understand women who don't want babies: what can it *really* be, what's wrong with them? You feel superior to them in your motherhood, despite everything that you've said about it.

Do not say that your children are people in their own right, that they can't help that you're their mum, and that their journey into the world is as valid as yours. Don't describe the smallness of their feet. It's not worth lingering on any new connections that kids forge between you and the rest of the world. Or the fact that, despite everything, your children like you, however your clothes look and smell. In fact they like you a lot more than your colleagues or even your friends ever have. But this may not last.

I once sat down to write in this vein, inhaling the indignation alongside the furious detractors and lid-lifters. I hadn't even advanced to the pay gap: my principal motivation was seeing that working mothers still do all the laundry. I have four kids and work part-time. Is it even possible, I wailed, at a lump of chisel-proof Weetabix, to be a mother and also write a book? How to battle the constant interruptions and the splintering of time, concentration and even your very own self?

I squinted back, with the distillation of radgy hindsight, into my teenage years. All those breezy assumptions about equality and worlds being oysters – how did they harden into resentment? Running headfirst into motherhood, that's how. I was a slow and reluctant adapter to the landscape of parenting, unwilling to acknowledge that the alien force known as babies can mark a profound change in women's lives. After having four of them, I'm still catching up with that identity split.

It first emerged long ago, on a night out with some work friends. We're in some place near Covent Garden, and the table's now covered in wine bottles. I'm the only one with babies. To rhyme with scabies and rabies. And I'm tired enough to feel delirious and have watery eyes, even though I'm only doing the odd freelance newsroom shift here and there. They are all caught up in the glamour of foreign news trips:

"Of course the Nigerian elections were *so* different this time round…"

"In Kabul we got so drunk the presenter fell in the swimming pool…"

"You wouldn't believe how many lines dropped in my outside broadcast…"

I sit through the evening with nothing to contribute. My week was spent going to and from Ten o'Clock Club, making playdough snails and pointing at trains. I get home that night in a state of anxiety, and tell Justin I don't like my friends any more.

He looks at me. "There's only one thing that you needed to say, and it would've stopped them in their tracks."

"What?"

"All you had to say was: I had an amazing morning, just playing with the kids."

"Hm. That's obnoxious," I say, grudgingly thinking he may be onto something. If this is true, it means that despite our current differences my friends and I have more in common than we thought. We share the same ailment: the feeling of being on the wrong part of the family-work continuum. The itch of constant reminders that there's always something else you should be achieving. But hasn't there been '70s feminism and "Having It All"? Who makes us feel this way? By which of course I mean: "Who can we blame for this?"

Whoever's nearest, usually. Resentment makes you say things that, as you say them, you notice make you sound like a right cow. But it's too late: it's already out there. "*Your* problem is that you're *too selfish* to pick the towel up off the floor, and now you're doing it just to *annoy* me," you shout, while your partner looks around for a towel that he wasn't even sure existed.

He doesn't know – and neither, perhaps, do you – that it may have taken a decade to build up the resentment centred on this towel. Or several centuries, if you count the simmering convoy of your female ancestors. There they are, glowering at the forlorn towel on the floor, grinding their medieval-teeth. To that towel, add the endless battles around affordable childcare and unequal wages.

Small wonder women are leaving it later before they take the motherhood plunge. But there's something they might not be seeing. There is another side: the joy in pulling it off. Wollstonecraft nailed it, way back in 1795. For all her torment, she was a skilled combiner of apparently conflicting forces in life. And following in her steps, I've made a discovery.

If you're doing work and parenthood without doing justice to either, then reassess. They might seem like two worlds at odds. But if you have any kind of toehold in both, that's something to celebrate. It's only a compromise if you think it is. I used to, but something changed when I followed Wollstonecraft to Norway. Instead of "Having It All", it feels more like just about getting away with it all.

Maybe doing some adventuring of my own addressed the resentment problem. Or maybe it was noticing too late how fleetingly baby time passes. But a notion that I've been hard-wired to scorn now has sudden urgency: it is possible eventually to get things like careers and social lives back. You will never get the baby time back.

Check me. One quick trip to Norway and suddenly I'm all Mrs Self-Help.

I'm back from the trip. It's taken a while to come back to writing, mostly because I couldn't bear for it to be over. I pre-savoured that journey for so long, imagining it on buses and in bed, planning it while walking to school. It became, in the friendliest of clichés, my dream come true. Now it's over. Clinging on is like trying to get back to sleep to re-enter a dream. It's fading, slipping away.

And that's not the only thing that's stopped me from writing. Don't think I haven't noticed the irony of writing about motherhood: if you're writing about it, you're not doing it. Result? Your writing's intermittent, and you're a crap mum too.

Anyway, I'm back. And here I was at my laptop innocently moving documents into new folders to make life more orderly, and there was that article by Virginia Woolf. It hooks me every time. Perfect like the ultimate strawberry: it is small, pungent, irresistible. I devour it:

The staple of her doctrine was that nothing mattered save independence. Independence was the first necessity for a woman – not grace or charm, but energy and courage and the power to put her will into effect.

Of the many examples of Wollstonecraft's independence, energy and courage, perhaps the most bonkers is when she takes off for Paris.

> she had put her principle of decisive action instantly into effect, and had gone to Paris determined to make her living by her pen.

Why? For the Revolution.

> The Revolution ... was not merely an event that had happened outside her: it was an active agent in her own blood. She had been in revolt all her life – against tyranny, against law, against convention.

My own blood speeds, pupils dilate, and it's time to get back out there. Back onto the rough invigorating seas of life in the company of the one and only Wollstonecraft. After all,

> as we read her letters and listen to her arguments and consider her experiments ... and realize the high-handed and hot-blooded manner in which she cut her way to the quick of life, one form of immortality is hers undoubtedly: she is alive and active, she argues and experiments, we hear her voice and trace her influence even now among the living.

I see these words and they hand me a new journey. Time to move again. I will go to Paris. Paris! I too will cut my way to the quick of life. Instead of the darkness of Risør, Paris is all the bliss of a new dawn. And it's not just political: it's a sexual dawning too. Cue Shaggy's 'Boombastic' intro; stand by for Mister Lover Lover. For it's here that she meets Gilbert Imlay.

Talking of blokes, should I take Will again? Part of me longs to scamper around on my own, not pushing a buggy with every flight of steps a barrier to progress and not having food thrown at me three times a day. But then, why make life easy when it could be complicated – and funny – and joyful? This is what I got from travelling with Will. It didn't make some parts better: it made everything better. He loved it, I loved him, he loved me, and everyone else loved us both. Typing this thought I have three times leapt up and paced the room in excitement and sat down again.

So, Paris it is. Paris with the baby. The baby and the discovery of a Third Way. I'm gradually convincing myself that, in trailing Wollstonecraft around, a mysterious enlightenment is taking place. Like Wollstonecraft, I too can merge the apparently polar opposites of family and career. I am on the brink of a breakthrough: two worlds becoming one. I'm doing this as a mother. As a Mother. Merging the hitherto exclusive spheres of my Venn-diagram existence. With the exception of these moments of writing furiously at my laptop, young Will is with me, and we're a team. We will go to Paris and prove it. This time I'm not nervous: I'm confident and clear.

"But what about your daughters – why can't they come along too?" a voice in my head demands. "No way!" I reply. I can't possibly do interviews with four kids milling around. What about that time I had to take them all with me to a meeting, and even though I bribed them with chips, just as I began to talk, Eva swung Elsa by the arm and then they all started to scream? "You've got a point," says the voice, "but that's your fault for having so many kids." "I agree, Voice, but who asked you? Aren't you the one that pops up every time my mothering isn't up to scratch? Like, take a hike, bud!"

Here I am, doing Scooby Doo impressions to a voice in my head. Never doubt that parenting bestows the ultimate panoply of transferable skills.

PART TWO

Chapter Nine

A Hopeful Feeling

Onwards to Paris. But everyone goes to Paris. It is the place to which writers must go. This puts me off. Hoping for inspiration I head down the local high street and into Kentish Town Library to check out the Paris guidebooks. They've all been borrowed. All of them? "Popular destination," remarks the librarian with a smile. "Everyone's going there: it must be the place to be… Maybe it's that Woody Allen film." He's obviously trying to wind me up.

Wollstonecraft was writing, while she was in France, her study of the Revolution. It's not much of a thriller, but even so her life was endangered by writing it. It's also not personal like the bursting and variegated *Letters from Norway*, which means it's going to be much harder to retrace her experiences. I need the services of a pro: I need Richard Holmes. That's *the* Richard Holmes; friend to the Romantics and a biographer among biographers.

Holmes is an old-school writer-in-Paris. He will have drunk pastis on a boulevard at the exact spot where Wollstonecraft cried out against the bloodshed of the Terror, I am certain. But according to his publisher, "Richard is busy working on another book and has no time for interviews". And my letter to him, invoking the earnest goodwill of a Wollstonecraft co-fanatic, remains unanswered.

I'm miffed. Not only was it his juicy introduction to *Letters from Norway* that got me into this whole thing, but he has "done" the Paris-in-another's-steps thing – and done it to perfection.

There is a strong element of the ridiculous in this Paris plan. First, a firebrand legend of a woman, the world's first feminist. In her footsteps, a clever biographer who looks like a spoof Englishman in round spectacles. Writing a book called *Footsteps*. And in their combined footsteps, there's me and Will, bouncing around grinning at each other.

Roberta the Wollstonecraft blogger comes round for some lunch. We eat toasted cheese sandwiches and I tell her about my Parisian anxieties. She listens kindly while I witter on, breaking off melty cheese bites for Will. She's also done the "Wollstonecraft in Paris" trip. Of course she has. What's more, she did it properly, taking a scholarly approach, and blogging this on her return:

> *I looked up Mary Wollstonecraft every way I could think of, and came up with a modest haul. From this I conclude that she didn't make much of a mark in France, partly because there were times during her sojourn when she had to lie low (Imlay registering her as his wife would only protect her so far, given that British citizens were personæ non gratæ once war was declared, and the couple had never been through a ceremony of marriage), and partly because there were so many momentous events going on, and so*

many distinguished foreign visitors, that her presence was
of small interest.

Not only is there nothing much there to find, but I'm joining
a whole crowd of ghosts, bumping into each other, frowning with the effort of soaking up some authentic Mary. Do I
mind following someone who is following someone else? Like
someone whose hobby is walking a few paces behind those
guys with metal detectors. Unlike Roberta, I don't even have
the metal-detector-like support of an archive of historical facts
or place references. I just have… a hopeful feeling.

And even that doesn't last. Compared to the Norway trip,
as this one looms closer, it reveals holes and fraying seams.
My attempts to contact people keep failing. Unlike helpful
Norway, Paris remains indifferent to my entreaties. They slip
through my fingers: famous feminists, interesting bookish
people. Even the hotel replies to my tentative "le petit-déjeuner,
c'est compris?" with a single word: "NON". I can't wimp out
now, though. Of course everything's been done before, and
written about brilliantly. But once we're there it'll make sense.
I recite once more:

A dish of coffee… recruited my spirits, and I directly set
out again…

Thinking back to the Norwegian rucksack blood-blisters, I
pack lightly this time, selecting my books with care. It's just
Will in his buggy in front and a small wheeled suitcase pulling
behind. It involves being a bit twisted and having no hands

free, but it's doable. We're like a small travelling circus, a three-part convoy, as we trundle our wheely way through St Pancras to the Eurostar.

We're going back in time, to before Wollstonecraft's treasure-hunting Norway trip. This is three years earlier. It's December 1792, and Wollstonecraft is thirty-three. She's a published woman and a noted thinker. She's also a virgin. But not for much longer. Her letters hint that she's keeping an eye out for some action. The eyes of the world, meanwhile, are on Paris: the very epicentre of human upheaval.

Wollstonecraft has just tangled with the prodigious Edmund Burke MP, and come out of it pretty well. Burke's snappily titled *Reflections on the Revolution in France, and on the Proceedings in Certain Societies in London Relative to that Event in a Letter Intended to Have Been Sent to a Gentleman in Paris* is an anti-Revolution bestseller. It defends "private property" and the "old institutions" against "unnatural" mob rule. He urges against copying, "in their desperate flights, the aeronauts of France". He praises chivalry, tradition and the British sense of knowing one's place. "All this violent cry against the nobility I take to be a mere work of art," he pronounces. "Fools rush in where angels fear to tread."

Our angel treads right up. She fearlessly bangs out the first among many responses to Burke, beating even Thomas Paine's legendary riposte. Wollstonecraft's *Vindication of the Rights of Men*, like much of her work, bursts out of her in one long angry breath. She demands to know

when you call yourself a friend of liberty, whether it would not
be more consistent to style yourself the champion of property.

She accuses him of supporting the slave trade: "a traffic that
outrages every suggestion of reason". She mocks him for suck-
ing up to the powerful and demolishes his "gallantry" with
arguments that will later become her *Vindication of the Rights
of Woman*. Though not averse to a dash of purple herself, here
Wollstonecraft skewers Burke's florid portrayal of the mob:

"Whilst the royal captives ... were slowly moved along,
amidst the horrid yells and shrilling screams and frantic
dances and infamous contumelies, and all the unutterable
abominations of the furies of hell, in the abused shape of the
vilest of women." Probably you mean women who gained a
livelihood by selling vegetables or fish, who never had had
any advantages of education.

Comparing Burke's arguments to the Hindu caste system, she
calls for people to be judged on their own merits. Given half
the chance, Wollstonecraft urges, even "the obscure throng"
can improve itself. "Virtue can only flourish among equals."
    And as always, she gets deliciously, extravagantly annoyed:

I pause to recollect myself, and smother the contempt I feel.

On first publication it's a well-received sell-out. It goes to a
second print run, but this time with her name on the front, and
the critics realize they're being lectured by an uppity woman.

This is where it gets ugly, and the "hyena in petticoats" mud-slinging begins. But her reputation is now made, and her name is out there. The ensuing pamphlet wars have the feel of a social-media storm: pamphlets too were cheap, fast and accessible. And the storm around the Revolution was all-engulfing. It's hard to underestimate the existential threat that many felt lapping at England's shores from just over the Channel.

Wollstonecraft brushes off inconvenient stories about prison massacres: it's the Revolution, and she must be there. She's also keen to escape an awkward love affair with a hot-tempered artist who already has a wife. So off she gallops, boasting in a letter:

> I have determined to set out for Paris ... and shall not now halt at Dover I promise you, for as I go alone neck or nothing is the word.

She also makes some teasing remarks about finding a hubby out there, then dumping him again. It doesn't quite happen like that though.

The first few days are tense and fearful. The acquaintances in whose house she's staying are away. She can't speak the language, and she misses her cat, and she daren't blow out the candle at night. She has a hallucinatory premonition of the Terror:

> Once or twice, lifting my eyes from the paper, I have seen eyes glare through a glass door opposite my chair, and bloody hands shook at me...

During this uncharacteristic wobble she even feels sorry for the King. The monarchy has fallen, but not yet been slaughtered. Witnessing Louis XVI passing in a carriage on his way to trial seems slightly to dent her faith in the Revolution. It may well be "the most extraordinary event that has ever been recorded", but up close to the blood-slippery pavements perhaps things aren't as clear-cut as they appeared from London.

So she's alone, and it's daunting in the extreme, but don't worry. This is Wollstonecraft. *Neck or nothing.* Up she springs, meeting people, soaking it up in revolutionary salons and learning French. She gets teased by an unnamed gentleman who warns her not to say "*oui oui*" too often. This silver-tongued rogue must surely be Imlay. And only a few months later the internationally-renowned author of *A Vindication of the Rights of Woman* will be pregnant.

Paris may be where she blossoms, produces and reproduces, but it's also the hardest place to track her – as Roberta found, there are so few textual clues. Unlike Norway, this won't lend itself to footstep-seeking. Our train pulls out through the gentle countryside. After a mighty struggle and a bellow, Will gives up the fight and falls asleep in my lap. I push my back into the velour Eurostar seat and make a decision: I'm not going to do any of that foot-stepping ghost-hunting stuff. I'm just going to find out the facts.

What was the Revolution, and what was it like to be inside it? Were the rights of women vindicated? And while we're at it, what about "*la condition féminine*" today? Back in my student texts, the French feminists were the world's most fearsome. These days they've got Dominique Strauss-Kahn.

Which supports my suspicion that it's not easy to be a French woman. You have to look good and be thin for starters, plus your hubby is likely to be a bit of a dog. That's me setting off with an open mind then.

Satisfied sigh and I look down at my boy and his peachy cheeks. I shift him around – my arm is going numb. I love his heavy form. After the battle to get him to sleep, I invariably get the urge to play with him and touch him. He's so soft, lying there. I lean as close as I can and sniff in his warmth – stare at him close up. He changes shape as he falls asleep: he seems to sink down and get longer. How clever that my elbow is a place to sleep, that my body makes a bed for him still. I get a tender sense of perfection and rightness that I can't properly explain. We doze.

Blink and you're already there. I love Eurostar, the most satisfying way to arrive in a city. We step lightly out of the Gare du Nord and walk straight down Paris, due south. It's a waste not to walk in Paris. And it's a good walk, taking in a sprinkling of African nail bars and groups of immigrants, as though a hint of the *banlieues* has made it downtown. Over the Seine, and here it is. Hotel Esmeralda. It's a small, quirky delight, with friendly Latino staff.

"Ah you are writing? Your English writer, Jeanette Winterson, she stayed here too." Hmm. No pressure then. We creak up some tiny wooden stairs that smell of polish and, I hate to indulge a stereotype, but onions – definitely onions and garlic. The room is old and funny: it feels like staying in a friend's aunt's house. We overlook a tiny pigeony park to the south of Notre Dame. Will has a cot and I have a bed – what more do we need? Maybe some food. Luckily this is Paris: we will dine like the gods every day.

Walking alongside the Seine to a play area with Will, I realize he's now in a different league of babyhood. If he's awake I can do very little apart from attend to his myriad and changing desires. We chase each other round a slide and kick up the yellow-gold leaves heaped round. I eagerly offer him the swings, but he runs back to the slide. I show him the roundabout, and he runs back to the slide. A shadow of dread falls across my mind: what if this slide is the only thing he'll approve of in the entire city?

Our first encounter is a feminist demo. Over the Seine and up to Place de la Bastille, the traffic is all cordoned off. Thousands of women from all over the country are uniting here to march across town, demonstrating about violence against women. Nosing Will's buggy through the campaigners, we negotiate a place near the front of a large group surrounded by banners. I catch myself noticing how well-groomed they all are, and smile guiltily at my neighbouring women. We hang about as more marchers gather. No one seems to wonder why I keep muttering into a Dictaphone. It's not a diverse crowd, and Will is the only bloke amongst us.

The group I've sidled up to and am now marching, indeed chanting with, is called *Osez le féminisme*. I ask one of them for an interview, and she agrees. Alice, like most of the marchers, looks like an office worker on her lunch break. She's a white, twenty-five-year-old blonde with a serious air. Alice tells me proudly that *Osez le féminisme* is only two years old but has over 1,500 members. "You are writing a book? What is it about?" She asks me with a steady gaze. "It's about what feminism means today," I say confidently. She narrows her eyes slightly and I hurry to my next question: why did she join up?

"There is an illusion of equality: we think that we are close, but equality is an illusion now. We have a country where 75,000 women are raped each year and only 2% of the rapists are condemned. We have salaries for men and women differing by up to 27%, so you can't speak about equality." Alice handles the data impressively. "The average age of our group is twenty-seven. We were born in the '80s and we have been educated into thinking that our grandmothers gained the equality, but now when we are on the labour market we discover that it's not the case."

"And when do we discover that it's not the case?" I ask. "Is it when women have children?"

"Yes, but men have children too," she asserts, not missing a beat.

"True, but…" I edge towards traitor territory, "but maybe there's a physical reason for women stopping working too, and some women want to—" I trail off.

"*Non.*" Her certainty is complete. "This can only explain why the firms act like this, it's an excuse. The maternity leave in France is four months, so how can we explain that men and women do not have the same salary? Four months in the life – it is nothing! You know: men can have cancer and leave their job for more than four months, but they are not discriminated against." I bet Alice gives it loads down the pub. This woman has no doubt. "Men and women must have access to the labour market equally. We are in a country now in France where 80% of domestic labour is done by women. How can we explain that?"

"Well how *can* you explain it?" I cut in. "Isn't there a chance that some of that, if it's childcare, is something people might love doing? Not the dishes obviously, but the good stuff. Maybe not all labour is… labour?"

"*Non* – they do it because of the patriarchy, and masculine domination. It has to change so that women can access the labour market in the same way that men do today. Discrimination has to stop, and we have to share domestic labour."

I can't help myself: "Aren't you worried about having babies?"

"I want to have babies, yes, but I'm not worried."

"You don't fear a change in your career or your position in society?"

"There is a risk, but that's why we want to change society – that is why we demand that our politicians and our president enforce real equality. We have formal equality, but now we need real equality."

Equality. Will and I peel off after three hours of chanting and marching, and I trundle us back along the streets of Saint-Germain-des-Prés, thinking about the labour market and domestic labour all the way. I very much like Alice and her twenty-five-year-old vigour, but it makes me feel suddenly aged. Part of me admires her; the rest is thinking: "Just you wait, love." Because it goes to the crux of why we don't have what Alice wants. It's those pesky babies.

If they arrived in the post, there'd probably be greater workplace equality. But they don't. They grow from scratch inside our bodies. That's pretty insane when you think about it.

Has this made me less enamoured of a life on the labour market? It's troubling that I might be a willing participant in what I previously considered inequality. But being in the new, ever-changing baby world instead of being out at work is not downsizing, and it's not downgrading. It's a different planet, incomprehensible to non-residents.

Occupying both planets simultaneously is a privilege. I don't want to compare my children to having cancer – a reason to lose four months on the labour market. I'm lucky to have my job and I'd go nuts without it. But the labour market does not have comically small feet, and it will never write me a love letter in smudged glitter-glue. Alice is not wrong. But the way she thinks is how I thought before kids. Maybe I'm further down the line from her. Maybe further down the line from me is a whole new something else.

Early the next morning I wake up before Will and sit quietly, contemplating the atrocious night from which I've just emerged. Hours lying there with my very soul churning in recollection of the food we've eaten. Where Wollstonecraft is haunted by nocturnal images of bloody fists, my nightmares are gastronomic. In fairness, we've been limited to places with baby chairs or buggy access. But even so. Top three offenders:

Curling-at-the-edges croque-monsieur with slopping centre of white cheese.

Molten dish of microwaved cheese with alleged core of pale lasagne.

Smelly grey chicken with damp chips.

Coming in a close runner-up was an improbably costly tray of dips, yoghurt and fruits in syrup. These Parisians are having a laugh. My stomach writhes and squeaks with these gurgling gastro-memories – but it's also fear. Fear that I'm wasting my time. I'm wasting time and money. Each time you sit down in Paris it costs about twenty euros. What's the point? What are we doing here?

It's unrealistic to try to get close to Wollstonecraft on this trip. I can't meander around in her pages, and we're not remotely in the same vein or life chapter. Last time we were both travelling with our babies, even if the similarity ended there. Here in Paris she is discovering great sex in the middle of the biggest political earthquake in history. I'm just a tired mum wandering about in a bad mood.

And Will's no longer the angel baby who charmed his way around Norway. He makes insistent noises like an alarm clock and head-butts me in the face. Will has become a toddler. He doesn't want to be in his buggy: he wants to be out, climbing things. He used to be pleasantly distracted if I let him play with my phone. Now he unlocks it and dials Emergency Call, laughing as I lunge to grab it back.

Truth is, I don't like toddlers. I mean of course I love *him*, but he's currently occupying the least adorable phase of childhood. Newborn babies all creamy and magical? Yes. Small-limbed children who say: "Mummy, I want to sleep in your hair"? Oh, yes. Swollen-headed anger machines who fall over all the time and can't wipe their own bums? No, thanks very much. Poor Will has become a challenge – an active impediment. I can barely interview people or look at anything for any length of time. All that stuff I said about how bringing a baby along makes everything easier and shinier and better? Big fat nonsense.

The Musée Carnavalet is the experience that brings it home. Will's had his breakfast, and I've timed it so he won't be tired. We arrive as soon as it opens, and I plan to go straight to the Revolution Rooms. I will take photos and make recordings of their Audio Guides, so that I can listen to and observe it all properly later. Fiendishly clever, I congratulate myself. But my carefully laid plans are no match for Will. I am asked to leave the buggy at the cloakroom, at the bottom of a sweep of marble stairs. I then carry my bag, camera, Dictaphone, audioguide and boy back up the stairs.

"The Revolution Rooms, *s'il vous plaît?*"

"Up two more flights of stairs madam, and along a corridor and upstairs again."

Oh great. I drag him up and get to the top pouring with sweat. He is bored already and wrestling in my arms. People laugh at us, and I decide that they are laughing in kindly sympathy. I set him gently down on the floor so he can steady himself, and a familiar meaty waft reeks out of his clothes. I don't believe it. All the nappy changing stuff is back downstairs in the buggy. We go back down again.

"Where can I change him?"

"In the toilets, *madame*, down the stairs."

Even more stairs? We smell the toilets before we see them. I look inside. No way. I change him right there in the middle of the stairs, almost urging someone to tell me off so I can ask how they'd like to lie down on that toilet floor. No one tells me off. I slam-dunk the heavy warm nappy into a bin, wash hands as Will scarpers out the door, sweep him into my arms and stomp all the way back up.

We make it, hot and flustered, back up to the Revolution Rooms, and the first thing I see is a miniature version of the Bastille. I put Will on the ground, take a photo and record some of the audioguide. As I'm doing this, Will totters round the corner, and I see the museum guards spring to life as they watch him lurch towards a priceless Revolution-era chair, once sat upon by a queen awaiting the guillotine.

"*Non madame*, he cannot touch!"

I pick him up again and try to look at a painting of Olympe des Gouges. Will head-butts me in the chest and shouts. I put him on the ground, and he runs off in a flapping penguin-like way, straight towards the original version of the *Declaration of the Rights of Man*, his fat hands outreached.

Another guard pops out. "*Madame, NON* – he must not touch it!"

"Well, can you stop him?" I bleat, knowing that's really not good enough.

And so it goes on. A sixteen-month-old child versus the collective might of the French Revolution. Room after room of things I can't look at properly; room after room of unsmiling guards. Mothers of toddlers will often get the feeling that people are staring disapprovingly, when they're probably not. But right now they definitely are. My arms are aching and my chest tightens. Finally I give up, and don't look at any exhibits at all, but merely follow in the random trail of my mini-dictator. "Quite another version of *Footsteps*," I think bitterly.

We get outside. Will chases a pigeon onto a lawn with signs saying something like "Babies Who Tread upon This Grass Will Be Decapitated", and I phone up Justin and burst into tears.

"This trip is rubbish! My whole idea is rubbish! You can't get stuff done with a baby after all!"

"Stick with it, Bee," he encourages, and I'm too upset to get indignant about his over-kindly tone. "Will was just bringing some authentic mob rule to the Revolutionary showcase. Sounds like he did a great job."

Chapter Ten

Allons enfants de la matrie,
le jour de gloire est arrivé

The next morning we set out with purpose and defiance. Paris, you won't get the better of us. For starters, the biggest twos-up I can think of is to have breakfast in Starbucks. Ha. It's reasonably priced. There's somewhere for Will to sit. And we can fill his baby cup with milk for free, instead of being charged €4 as per everywhere else. This morning is about *droits du bébé* as well as *droits de l'homme*. I smirk at the city as we emerge, caffeine-charged and ready for action. "A dish of coffee" recruits our spirits once again. Today we will get some answers. Answers to questions like: the Revolution, what was that all about?

Hannah Callaway does tours for Context Travel, a tour-guide agency for clever rich people. Today she's making a charitable exception. Hannah is a New Yorker, researching her Harvard PhD on the French Revolution here in Paris. She's primarily interested in Tom Paine. I don't begrudge him. His life story makes even Wollstonecraft's look pedestrian. How can you resist a carpenter who becomes a global political rockstar – the daddy of not one, but two revolutions – then ends up dying a pauper's death in New York?

The Norfolk lad turned American founding father isn't only a key figure here in Paris, but also in Wollstonecraft's private life. The first time she meets her future love, the philosopher William Godwin, they've come to a dinner back in London to hear the celebrated and notorious Paine speak. But he doesn't get a word in edgeways, because Wollstonecraft won't shut up. This pricelessly crap first date is later described by Godwin:

> *The interview was not fortunate. Mary and myself part-ed mutually displeased with each other. I had not read her Rights of Woman. I had barely looked into her An-swer to Burke... I had therefore little curiosity to see Mrs Wollstonecraft, and a very great curiosity to see Thomas Paine. ... The conversation lay principally between me and Mary. I, of consequence, heard her, very frequently when I wished to hear Paine.*

Hannah has wayward mid-brown hair, unruly eyebrows and busy eyes. We smile and introduce each other, shaking hands formally. She is warm and keen to help, but she isn't much of a one for small talk. Within very few seconds she is telling me, as I gulp down the last of my rebellious Starbucks, that "Rous-seau's vision of the formation of government and the way that democratic government should work differs from a more Anglo-American view. That is, Rousseau focused on the gen-eral will, and so the idea is that everyone comes together over a consensus that emerges from political discussion. Whereas the Anglo-American tradition emphasizes contention within politics, where dissent is not only allowed but expected, and is built into the system. So that our system envisions that there will be conflicting views, and it tries to balance them out – and that's the classic theory of the American Constitution. While the French idea of general will is that politics is essentially consensual. So there is a problem when you have people with dissenting views, because either they must be against the common interest or they must be wrong. There's no way to envision that they could potentially be correct if they're the voice of the minority. So. Let's get started with the Bastille, as we are standing right here".

I inspect my coffee dregs, wishing for an extra shot. It's barely nine o'clock and she's speaking in rapid-fire paragraphs without commas. I decide not to mention coming as a student to see the Bastille, only to find it was no longer here. How cheated I felt that it's now basically a roundabout. We stand at the brink of the screeching traffic.

"It's wild," she says. "I'll show you: over here we can see in the paving stones the outline of the Bastille. If we cross the street, here you can see it comes all the way across, then over there, look, there's another one. These are the imprints of the outer turrets, occupying this entire space."

Hannah sweeps an arm around as we teeter on the edge of the vortex of cars and buses swerving past Will's buggy. Stepping back from the pavement edge she continues: "If you steal a loaf of bread and you're convicted and put in jail, you don't go to the Bastille, you go to a regular prison. People who go to the Bastille are different – they're imprisoned at the King's will. Or they could also be imprisoned by a *lettre de cachet*."

"Elettra de Who?"

"A *lettre de cachet* – it's a document that any man, any father of a family in France can get issued against a member of his family. So if your son is wasting your fortune with gambling debts, or he won't marry the right person, you can get the King to throw him in the Bastille."

"And only fathers could do it?"

"Only fathers, or the King. So the reasoning is that the King is the father of the country, and every family is modelled on the monarchy, because every father is a little king." She enjoys my horrified look. "They're all mini-kings, yeah. And what the Bastille symbolizes for the people is the arbitrary power of the absolute monarchy. So it has an extremely strong symbolic power."

Clever Americans tend to talk faster than clever people from elsewhere. Hannah's no exception, but she is so absorbed into her subject that it's contagious. People and traffic flow past us as we wander along, talking quickly, walking slowly. She constructs the living, seething Revolution all around us as we go. Hannah's face is young, but she has wisps of grey in her hair. This is pretty revolutionary too, given the rigour of Parisian standards of feminine grooming.

"People begin to gather up and they march to the Bastille. The Bastille is now surrounded by people, and the word is spreading. Rumours flow in decentralized ways. Women are key to this. They are important vectors of information: they are out in the streets, they're in the markets, they are out circulating."

I can't help smiling at women being "important vectors of information". They were the French Revolution's Facebook.

"In these situations it's always hard to know exactly who started what, where and how. But suddenly the guards begin firing, the people begin attacking and nearly everyone inside is killed. The governor is brought outside, and his head is cut off. They stick the head on a pike, and they march it around as a sign of victory, as a symbol. The Revolution co-opts a lot of the ritualistic violence of the Ancien Régime. But I want to shift off the narration of this event and give you a larger sense of where other things are fitting in."

Hannah's right – the threads are too multiple, too enticing. Plus, she keeps getting faster as the story becomes more blood-soaked. I tell her I'm hoping to learn how it would have been for Wollstonecraft, and how the Revolution did or didn't help women.

"Wollstonecraft doesn't really mention women in her writing here, apart from being pretty horrified by the 'female mobs'..."

"Yes, the women's movement," Hannah says. "Inasmuch as there is such a thing. On the general stage we have the popular movement and the elite movement, and it's the same with the women. Women don't have one unified point of view, and they don't have a unified point of action. So on the one hand we see hungry women marching for bread, and on the other these aristocratic women hosting salons. So it's one of these tricky things where it looks like maybe women are being treated as equal, but..." She pauses.

"In a girly way?"

"Yeah, they're being valued, they're doing something important, but what they're contributing is something distinctly feminine. That's the idea: they're feminine characteristics, so it's not equal, because they are different. This is a tricky thing."

"It's still a tricky thing, equality... and difference..." I stare back along the street. Hannah is looking at me quizzically.

"Do you have kids?" I ask.

"No."

Screeching gear change as I hastily return us to the Revolution: "So the optimism of the movement, which captivates the Romantics back in England, it goes way beyond getting bread for hungry people, doesn't it?"

"You have to realize what they were up against. We are talking about the monarchy, which has become absolute by the time of the Revolution, and a caste system that has been in place, to use their language, since time immemorial. Authority stems from tradition. And this is the fundamental point of the Enlightenment: moving away from the argument of tradition and instead saying no: you know what, we are going to interrogate tradition, and we are going to bring it up against reason. And if it's not rational, it doesn't matter if it's been around for thousands of years – we're going to get rid of it."

"Reason!" I light up. "Wollstonecraft bangs on about the importance of Reason all the time. Somehow it never really struck me as all that much to ask."

"OK, this is *so* important, because that's the discourse of the Enlightenment that she's using. Reason is man's capacity, through rationalism and logic, to determine what is right. It's saying we can figure out answers for ourselves. *That* is revolutionary. Wollstonecraft is saying: I am a rational being, because I can *use my reason*. Of course I can, because look at me: I'm doing it – right? And people argued at the time women were not even capable of using reason – that they only had sloppy sentiment. So reason is doubly important for her than for male writers. And this is what's kind of heart-breaking – you see in the Revolution that women take action: they march for bread, they act as citizens, and they simply behave as equals. But the male revolutionaries who are in power ultimately reject that. And this happens on both levels: both to the elite women and also within popular politics—"

"Why, why did they?" I cut in, upset.

"Why did women behave as citizens?"

"No. Why did the male revolutionaries reject them?"

"Let me explain within the context." Hannah says. I stifle an impatient sigh: can't there just be a reason? "There is, of course, a lot of good intention. On the legislative side, the Republic is declared in September 1792, and laws start being passed right away. Divorce is legalized. And there's huge uptake. There's also a law on equal inheritance for men and women. But in a few years Napoleon takes over. In 1805 divorce becomes illegal again, and there's a conservative back-lash against the Revolution that's going to have a huge impact on women. They end up being trapped in that backlash that reasserts very traditional values."

Divorce is a subject close to Wollstonecraft's heart. The rule of law could safeguard women's very lives. These days it's sometimes an excuse for couples to tear chunks off each other while their lawyers make a fortune. But in her time, a husband quite literally owned his wife – could take her assets and have her imprisoned at will, take away her kids and abuse her with impunity. Marriage is a nightmare, haunting all of Wollstonecraft's writings like a crouching dark demon. She is rightly terrified of it.

We're now walking along the Rue de Rivoli, and I ask if we can sit on the grass in the Tuileries to let Will stretch his small legs. He's been patiently sitting in his buggy throughout the tempestuous tutorial. Over his unbothered golden head we've discussed the Jacobin Club, the bread marchers, the King's attempt to flee dressed as a servant and war with the crowned heads of Europe. We're in our own revolutionary bubble on the bustling streets.

"I still don't understand." I say, popping Will's seatbelt open and unleashing him onto the grass. "I get the backlash, but not why the revolutionaries themselves failed to go further at the time – why couldn't women be considered as equals?"

"OK. Take slavery. There is slavery in the French colonies. And as we see later in America, the question of women's suffrage and of blacks becoming full citizens comes up at the same time. And this is what happens in the Revolution: the question of freeing slaves and the question of women's rights are also being posed."

"What, then it was just too much freedom to handle?"

"You can see that the revolutionaries are trying so hard, but the new world is very much their own vision. The new possibilities are very specific in terms of their own political and economic freedom. Consider the commercial value of the French colonies and sugar islands like Haiti. So when other groups, like slaves, get excited too and say: 'Hey, OK, freedom

– let's do it!' suddenly it goes beyond what they had originally envisaged, and they are afraid."

We go quiet for a moment. Will runs over and urgently bestows a hedgerow leaf on me, pressing it into my hand before wobbling away. Cheered, I bring the conversation back to my guiding star. Wollstonecraft arrives fairly late on into the Revolutionary action. It's November 1792, only a few weeks after the founding of the New Republic and these new laws. Other Romantic thrill-seekers like Wordsworth are already leaving in fear. In fact, Wordsworth flees in the very same week that Wollstonecraft arrives (abandoning his pregnant girlfriend on the way – oh, those revolutionary men).

"Wollstonecraft's arrival pretty much coincides with the start of the Reign of Terror, doesn't it?"

"OK – so the Terror is very specific, and it starts after the monarchy falls. The King is arrested in August 1792, after a dramatic invasion of the Tuileries. But the Republic isn't declared until September. Meanwhile a rumour spreads that the prisons of Paris contain foreign conspirators. A group of *sans-culottes* go into the prisons, and they just slaughter over a thousand trapped prisoners. It's extraordinarily bloody and totally bizarre. And it's dreadful. There's no way of justifying it: it's dreadful."

We sit.

"And this is when we get the stuff from Dickens: the guillotine, the knitters, the countless tumbrels – and all the time they're hacking people's heads off willy-nilly?"

"Yes." Hannah says quietly. "Literally thousands of people have their heads chopped off."

Madame la Guillotine. Funny they didn't mind allowing gender in there. The machinery is female. As is the statuesque embodiment of la Liberté. Idealized abstract females are celebrated – but real, actual women popping up and demanding stuff? Er – no, we're all right, thanks.

We've wandered at meandering Will-speed between hedgerows of the Tuileries, and now, sitting on the grass, we're cold. Hannah suggests a coffee. We capture Will, and like the women bread marchers bringing the King on a cart back to Paris, take him to the nearest café. Hannah opens the door, and the warm air meets us. We sit down inside; my nose is dripping and my microphone hand has frozen. Will's cheeks are red, and he's hungry. The welcome glory of coffee and a cheese omelette arrives at the table. Over the noise of cutlery and sweeping waiters, Hannah summarizes:

"Women in the Revolution were deemed to have this special sympathetic power that can civilize men. The emerging sense is that home is the women's domain. It's the woman who is full of love and care, the woman who is the source of virtue and morality—"

The omelette wolfed, Will starts reaching out for things to grab and pull towards him, like a human whirlpool. He throws a spoon and the menu as we hastily move the Dictaphone, the salt and pepper, then our phones, and then our coffee away from his angering reach.

"But when women start taking action," she goes on "saying: 'All people are born equal' and joining in and taking part, the Jacobins become startled and say: 'What are you doing here?!' – and they just ignore them—"

Will rubs his eyes, then suddenly starts to sob. "I know – can you *believe* those Jacobins?" I say emphatically. He doesn't think it's funny. He's put up with a lot today: the omelette was my last trick. With no other distractions it's time to call it a day. I'm grateful that Hannah spoke so quickly, that we could fit so much into the time we had. We hug warmly and say our goodbyes. I load Will into his buggy, blanket him up and lie him down flat for his well-earned sleep, and we set off back down the Rue de Rivoli.

I'm stunned and aroused by this gale-force encounter. A respectful love for Paris surges inside me. They may not have baby chairs in restaurants, but modern civilization began right here. The keys to history are all around us as we hurry along, weaving through glossy shoppers and tourists. I breathe it in and feel small. Here on these streets, among the history-drenched symbols and monuments. A nod to the statue of Joan of Arc, wielding her golden flag in the air. I gaze up, indulging a daydream that one day, maybe one day, there will be a statue of Wollstonecraft.

Passing yet another Starbucks, I'm struck by a rueful thought. Not only did we enjoy an insolent American breakfast this morning, I've also just done the French Revolution with an American, albeit a Francophone one. It feels remiss. We need to boost the intake of proper Frenchness. Luckily I've found a source of *appellation d'origine contrôlée*. He is an expert in the Revolution from the University of Paris, and he's suggested we meet in a café on the Quai de Loire, near to his campus. *Allons-y*. Will and I catch the metro to Stalingrad in the 19th Arrondissement.

Professor Marc Belissa is in his fifties, with dark hair. He's tall and smokes roguishly. He does that French thing of being more attractive than he actually is. How do they do that? We sit down to black coffees with Will pulled up between us. I stir my coffee with the plastic thing that isn't a spoon, and get the recording equipment ready. It's kind of him to come and meet us, but from the outset he's quite sniffy about Wollstonecraft. He says there's not much interest in her in France, adding vaguely: "They probably do like her in the US and the UK, though."

He delivers this snub so enchantingly that I find myself smiling along. Maybe it's his accent. Then he asks me if I know much about the Revolution. I flash back to my head-spinning time with Hannah, and tell him I've learnt there are no short cuts, but that I'm keen to discover how life would have been for a foreigner living here during Revolution, and especially during the reign of Terror.

"Ah," he intones. "You have to make the distinction between the first three years of the French Revolution, 1789 to 1792, and the so-called period of Terror, which I call the period of the Revolutionary Government. Because that is the real name of this period. I don't call it 'the Terror'. The word Terror, it's not very precise. What is Terror? Is it a series of practices? Is it a programme? If you look carefully, you see that the Terror was never proclaimed – there was never a law. There was not a 'Reign' or 'regime' of Terror!"

"Oh, come on, all that blood-letting," I say, "and the general state of paranoia?"

"It's not paranoia when it's *real*," he insists, calling to mind a Hollywood blockbuster. "And as for the blood? That was also there in 1789, and you don't call 1789 the Terror. France was very isolated – France was at war with nearly everyone: she fought her neighbours because they had declared hostility to her. It was war! The radicalization of the French Revolution *cannot* be understood without the context of the war – it's a *European problem*."

"But what about the machinery of Terror – I mean, literally a machine for publicly chopping off lots of heads?"

"*Non.*" Professor Belissa decapitates my question. "Terror is not a machinery: it's a slogan. It's not a regime and it's not a philosophy. You have to think of the Terror as also the most democratic period of the Revolution: you have to think at the same time of both democracy and Terror, which is quite difficult." He utters the word distinctly, and it's definitely Terror with a capital T.

"During the Terror, slavery was abolished in France. During the Terror, the right to existence was proclaimed in the 1793 *Droits de l'Homme*. During the Terror, the widows got pensions from the state. The poor and the women without husbands got social legislation – that was all during the Terror. So if you see it uniquely in terms of bloodshed, then you don't understand all the social advances."

Right. This isn't giving me much of an angle on how it was to be Wollstonecraft, arriving just as Wordsworth scuttled back to English safety. I try to steer us back to being a foreigner coming here in 1792. How might you be treated?

"That depends which country you're from. If you're American it's OK. If you think in terms of who was farthest away on the scale of liberty, at the bottom was the Spanish. For the French, even before the Revolution Spain was considered backwards. It was a place where priests dominated. Italy also, because of the power of the Pope. The Belgians, they had a revolution at the same time as us, but it was ended in 1790 by Austrian repression and the Hapsburg monarchy. But to be English was maybe the worst you could be. And this is not because they were the worst enemy. *Non*. This is because they were seen as the people who *should have been* the natural allies of the Revolution. They knew about the *Rights of Man*, they had a limited monarchy, they had political parties and the English liberty – so those people should have been sympathetic. And so the Revolutionaries saw the English as the worst enemies of all, because they betrayed us."

I note the word "us". And the disdain for the English. But Professor Belissa is impossible to dislike. I persist: "Wollstonecraft's boyfriend is American and has certain privileges, and for her safety he registers her as his wife even though they're not really married. So at what point did it become a danger to her life to be English rather than just an affront to people?"

"Your country was at war with my country, remember. The legislation passed a law that all citizens of countries at war with France had to be watched. English people were banned from Paris and from border and port towns. For Tom Paine there was of course an exception: he was naturalized. But at one point the French thought it was necessary to expel all foreigners – Paine included. And when Paine came out of jail, he said: 'I understand these measures – even if they were harsh, I understand it was necessary.' So people like Paine and Wollstonecraft were considered suspect in terms of being foreigners, but not really as criminals. People think: 'Ah, Paine was in jail, so France must be chauvinistic.' But it's not true."

Far from Hannah's account of the French political paradigm being all about consensus, Professor Belissa is relishing this debate, and the more I question his Revolution, the more he enjoys himself.

"Are you defending the Revolution?"

"No. I'm defending complexity. There is no neutral language. We must see that the term 'Reign of Terror' was invented in 1795, after the Terror, by the people who killed Robespierre and blamed everything on him. He was a scapegoat. He was not bad – all of them were... It's a complete misunderstanding."

"Are you saying Robespierre wasn't guilty of crimes?"

"But were they crimes? Is it a crime to execute people for being counter-revolutionary, in a Revolution? It's only three thousand—"

"*Only* three thousand?!"

I go into Gallic gesticulation overdrive, nearly falling off my chair. Professor Belissa is unruffled: "You have to compare it to the thousands and thousands of French dying in the armies along the way. And all those dying of hunger? Not during the Terror. During the Terror the price of bread was protected and no one died of hunger. There was famine *after* the Terror; in 1795 the Seine froze over, a lot of people died, bread was very expensive and crops failed. What about these deaths, ah?"

Will starts to wrestle around in his buggy, and I am quite relieved. For once his timing is welcome, as there's nowhere else to go. It's come down to head-chopping: for or against. So I ask if we can walk around outside to distract Will. Professor

Belissa doesn't mind at all: he jumps up and gallantly holds the door open for us. As we step outside, I ask a question that is probably rather pointless at this stage. But I can't help myself:

"What about the women of the Revolution?"

"Obviously it's complicated," he says. Well fancy that. "You can see this period as a moment when women took the power to speak, to say things, and to demand things."

"But they didn't seem to get them. Or even if they did, it was rolled back afterwards, like the divorce laws."

He executes a perfectly delicious French shrug and ignores this, continuing: "But you can also see it as a period in which the women were excluded from political life. Some historians, especially the Americans and feminists, they see it in this way."

"And those 'Americans and feminists', are they right or wrong?"

"Both!" he says with delight.

Chapter Eleven

How Not to Betray the Light?

This slightly maddening encounter has provoked more questions than answers. The defence of complexity is worthwhile in principle, but the struggle for simplicity strikes me as a whole lot more useful. Professor Belissa lights a cigarette and walks us to the Metro, exuding elegant smoke and chatting away merrily. I've enjoyed meeting him very much, but can't help wondering what he made of it. But then… a British Wollstonecraft fanatic with a baby. What did he expect?

Later on I am still reflecting on Professor Belissa and his apparent ease in accepting the price of the Revolution. Perhaps he's right that the blood-soaking and distracting violence has stopped me from seeing the good that happened. Wollstonecraft is harrowed by the violence: she publicly cries out at the sight of the blood-stained street. She makes such a fuss that she herself is at risk: concerned bystanders hurry her away to safety. Her once-pumped enthusiasm now tempered, she writes:

Every political good carried to the extreme must be productive of evil.

But then, she is right here at the heart of it all, escaping the old ways and traditions. Here at the decapitation of the Ancien Régime, the birth of the values of modern civilization.

Unprecedented freedom is springing up all around her. And freedom has unforeseen consequences: it is also freedom for your enemy. William Blake, the Enlightenment's own illustrator, knows this when he says of Milton's *Paradise Lost* that Milton is "of the devil's party without knowing it".

And maybe it's bloody, but what's the alternative? Back home Wollstonecraft has some powerful enemies. England, so recently the scene of that magnificent ding-dong between Wollstonecraft and Burke, is now in full backlash mode. The suspicion she arouses as a foreigner in France pales beside the hostility she would face if she returned. She's not welcome in England. The vibrant debate of 1792 is annihilated in repressive measures bearing names like the Aliens Act and the Treason Trials.

The 1793 Aliens Act is the government's response to the thousands of refugees (or émigrés, for your posh refugees: several noted Marquises and Chevaliers become waiters and window cleaners in their new English lives) fleeing the Revolution in France. This legislation requires all arrivals from France to register with the authorities, and failure to do so means imprisonment without trial. On top of the suspension of habeas corpus, prohibitive taxes are imposed on pamphlet publishing, and large public gatherings are banned. Anything to squash public interest in the shockwaves emerging from France.

The 1794 Treason Trials are an especially ugly expression of establishment fear. Growing numbers of people, inspired by the French, have begun to call for a more representative government, and an end to MPs buying their titles. The most outspoken are accused of revolutionary tendencies. They are spied upon and harassed by the government. They are arrested, and in a hearty assertion of proper traditional values, they face being hung, drawn and quartered. Even when acquitted, the defendants are crucified by the press.

Wollstonecraft's luminous circle of radical friends is surrounded by darkness. Her oldest champion and supporter, the big-hearted publisher Joseph Johnson, gets caught in the crush. Despite having published works on both sides of the revolutionary divide, Johnson is thrown in prison and thereafter sticks to the safety of publishing Shakespeare. Tom Paine is tried and found guilty *in absentia*. William Blake ends up in court on trumped-up charges of treason.

This anti-revolutionary bonfire consumes many, including Johnson's close friend Joseph Priestley. Priestley is cut from the same eccentric, self-made cloth as Wollstonecraft. A Yorkshire chemist and preacher, he speaks seven languages, discovers oxygen and tries to reinvent Christianity. He also accidentally creates fizzy drinks, which a certain Mr Schweppe then exploits to make a fortune. When he joins the call for political reform, his house is burnt down, he is savaged in the press and his family is attacked. He eventually flees to America.

If people like these are having their effigies burned at the stake back in England, then no wonder France feels forward-looking. Wollstonecraft's *Historical and Moral View of the Origin and Progress of the French Revolution* defends the Revolution's principles, but suggests with a sigh that the French just aren't ready. Looking back over the Channel she must have spotted that the French don't own the intellectual property rights over Terror. When she gets offered a safe passage home in the darkest hour, Wollstonecraft has no intention of heading back. *Non, merci.* She will take her best chances here with the Revolution, in all its messy hopefulness.

I promised not to do any ghost-hunting, but I can't help myself. Thanks to Richard Holmes we easily find the address where Wollstonecraft lived on first arriving here in Paris. It's 22 Rue Meslay, just off the Place de la Republique. This is the place where she has the spooky visions, keeps the candle alight all night and misses her pet cat. These days the house is a shirt shop. In a narrow, ordinary street full of other shirt shops.

The shop window is packed with special offers: three shirts for 30 Euros. As we stare in, an aspiring young accountant carrying a plastic bag steps out of the door. He's wearing – good grief – those slip-on loafers with a tassle. How could he know that his ill-shod footsteps are blaspheming hallowed ground? Tread softly, because you tread on my hero. The stiffly folded shirts are wrapped in cellophane, and they range all the way from white to very pale blue. This is even less atmospheric than Yoga Lady's bathroom in Kragerø.

I ask a passer-by to take a photo of me and Will smiling awkwardly in front of the shirt shop. It's all a bit rubbish. But there is good news: a détente has been reached between us and Parisian food. Seasoned travellers that we are, Will and I have taken to buying a few essentials and dining on park benches. It's a high-risk enterprise in November, but with surprising dividends. We have the best bread, the best cheese and unparalleled views.

A swift assessment of the benches generally reveals the same availability: every bench has one person sitting in the middle, with strategic bags and/or coat placed either side to occupy the space. Will and I gradually formulate the following counter-occupation algorithm:

1) Select the most bureaucratic-looking bench-dweller on offer (NB: not eccentric whiskery types who might start a conversation or people in twos who won't notice).
2) Plonk myself down right next to him.
3) Start singing at Will in a nauseating mummy voice.
4) Within roughly three minutes we have our own bench.

Paris has another park every few steps: once you start looking and if you're not too choosy there's no end of them. Our hard-won benches are the ideal place to watch Paris and its people streaming past, each wrapped in a private lunch-break drama. I indulge in the traditional scorn of the tourist towards other tourists. We of course look far more authentic and local: look at us – we're eating cheese. There's a steady supply of enthusiastic pigeons to feed or chase, depending on Will's mood. Some chocolate mousse and a "borrowed" teaspoon, and we're in heaven.

Beside us, under a neighbouring bench, a brown cluster of sparrows swoops down. Piaf! I haven't seen these for ages, since the inexplicable sparrageddon wiped them from Britain's city streets. I watch them bouncing about in the dust. Why do you insist on hopping? Can't you evolve and learn to walk? No wonder you're facing extinction. Get a grip, sparrows. Check out the pigeons, larging it, eating and shagging all over town. And walking. Even the ones with no feet. That's how you conquer an urban landscape. I throw a chunk of baguette and they descend on it, squabbling.

Among the flow of passers-by and birds there's time and space to reflect, and to realize the extent to which I've blithely crowbarred the concerns of my own life into the encounters we've had. Looking back, Norway was a giddy abandonment of domesticity. But this trip has leant back towards the theme, testing and poking it, holding it up to the pale-yellow Parisian light to see whether it alters somehow.

Having babies seems to make us different. Is this a good thing or something we should ignore? Where does motherhood fit into a revolutionary landscape? What is there, in the space between Hannah's Jacobins saying "Home is the woman's domain" and Alice's equality, where maternity is equal to four weeks' sick leave for cancer? I'm still not sure.

Will eyes me while I lick the lid of the chocolate mousse.

We still have two Parisian days left, and there is no one else to talk to but Will. I'm quite glad. My head is filled with the apparently conflicting spheres of domesticity and Revolution. Will and I hang out in the kids' end of the Jardin du Luxembourg: I push him on at least a hundred different swings, and we play among the golden leaves.

Around Will I read, with a rare and hungry devotion. The immersive effect of reading is very much deepened by being foreign – even more so by being a bit lonely. When Will has a nap and when he nods off in his travel cot at night, I rush to find my page. *Footsteps: Adventures of a Romantic Biographer* by

Richard Holmes. My own footsteps have drawn an uncertain wobbly circle. His are confident: his footsteps are strides.

Holmes heads here to revolutionary Paris as a young man drawn to the 1968 student uprising. He gets up close to the febrile anti-establishment fervour, with its massive demos, barricades and rifle-wielding troopers crushing down the young and the hopeful. Only one literature can describe this: "What I was feeling, and what my friends were feeling, seemed to be expressed perfectly by the Romantics, and no one else."

He goes on: "The whole ethos of the Sixties – that youthful explosion of idealism, colour, music, sex, hallucinogenic states, hyperbolic language and easy money ... was based on a profoundly romantic rejection of conventional society, the old order, the establishment, the classical, the square..."

Like Wollstonecraft, Holmes arrives once the action is well underway, and he watches for long enough to get a sense of its unravelling. Disillusionment follows, in "communes that went broke, free unions that became bad marriages, university faculties that became hotbeds of rivalry, artistic spirits who became addicts and breakdowns, travellers who came home sick and sorry, women who became exhausted one-parent families, a world of little presses and alternative newspapers that dropped into oblivion, and a Paris where the Bourse remained and Les Halles was destroyed."

Reading this I get an uncomfortable feeling. It's going to happen all over again, isn't it? Will there always be an equal and opposite reaction – a Napoleon for every Paine? Will the beautiful young renegades keep selling out or getting squashed in the backlash? It's not easy to keep the

Wollstonecraft fires burning. As Holmes asks: "How not to betray the light?"

And it's the pursuit of answers to these very questions that brings Holmes here on his *Footsteps* mission. This is how he finds Wollstonecraft, his "guide".

"There was something … like a wild waterfall in the headlong, broken, plunging quality of Mary's life. I stood and gazed at it roaring through the streets of Paris, visible only to me."

Let me see! I lean up against my guide, looking over his shoulder, trying to glimpse this roaring waterfall visible only to him. The waterfall escapes me, but the proximity is seductive. He's never boring, and we only have a couple of tiffs. Once when he portrays her transformation into motherhood as a shrinking act. He whittles her world down to three people in a room, a narrow cameo of the nuclear family. You can hear the disappointment:

"She who had prided herself, for half a lifetime, on her independence, her vocation as a writer, her revolutionary duty to her fellow women, was now committed to achieving and sharing domestic happiness of the most traditional kind."

Even if you accept these two states as necessarily exclusive, the bar seems to be set higher for women writers. The slightest perceived deviation in their private behaviour and all credibility is at stake. (Have male authors endured such scrutiny? Dickens had several hundred kids and no one suggested he might stop writing.) Yes, Wollstonecraft spends time in Neuilly and Le Havre. So would you if you were an illegal alien with the guillotine in full swing. What matters is that she doesn't resign or recant: she's still writing.

Even more annoyingly, Holmes credits Imlay with giving Wollstonecraft a new voice, greater insight, better writing. This is not right. It's true that she retreats into domesticity. Maybe she even enjoys it – and why the hell not: may the indignant lightning of liberation strike me down. And behold: she then emerges with a new voice. Old Quickfire McShoot-'em-up is replaced by the personal honesty of *Letters from Norway*. It's a new kind of writing. But this is not thanks to Imlay. It's thanks to the baby.

This isn't to argue that motherhood begets uniquely searing artistic sensibility. Take Emily Brontë, George Eliot, Zora Neale Hurston, Harper Lee and Virginia Woolf, to name a few. No, it's not like squeezing out a sprog can instantly genius you up. But it's a creative act and can be useful as such. I spent a decade of motherhood pretending it hadn't made the slightest difference, working in a newsroom for God's sake. You're not even supposed to smile, let alone cry or have passions or be convulsed with the love of fellow humanity. But why not give free rein to that new, forever-raw nerve?

Enough ungrateful squabbling: Holmes is a maestro. He brings me closer to Wollstonecraft, and I longingly savour the art of his pages. He fancies her too, and that makes me fancy him: we are an experimental Wollstonecraftian ménage. Me and Mister Holmes, we've got a thing going on. Even though we've never met.

How can you not love a writer so dedicated that he gets trapped, entangled in veg-patch netting as he attempts an illicit poetry reading in the same location it was written? He escapes by climbing a pear tree. I sense his mistrust of arrogant long-haired Saint-Just types, and share it, more than I initially realize.

Holmes draws a straight line from the French Revolution to the uprising of 1968. He links the Romantics to the hippy generation's free love and flower power. That movement, too, is "international: the counter-culture took to the road and passed all frontiers, entered all cities; just as the first Romantics had set out on their wanderings". As he leaves Wollstonecraft behind and moves on with her next generation, the Romantic offspring, my doubts will soon be reinforced.

The Wollstonecraft gene pool is such a catalogue of bleakness, it seems to be cursed. The first-born daughter, Frances, is now dead. That mini sidekick on the Scandinavian adventure, whose flushed cheeks and pattering footsteps lifted her mum's heart? She has succeeded where her mother failed and committed suicide. Hers are the baby steps that my Will retraces. But the "little frolicker", lavishly adored and written about by her mother, dies a lonely death by laudanum in a Welsh hotel room. She is buried, unacknowledged, in a pauper's grave.

The remaining descendent is Mary Shelley, and she forms one third of the travelling circus of misery and death that Holmes describes in the next stage of his *Footsteps*. Mary Shelley, her husband Percy, and her stepsister Claire Clairmont, plus their assorted children and visitors, are hoboing around Italy taking residences here and there. These children of the Revolution wander, fleeing debtors and the outrage of their own families, onwards in search of the Golden Age.

They are stalked by death. Mary Shelley, a teenage mum with no mother of her own, suffers the loss of three children.

The first child, Clara, dies shortly after her premature birth. The next, Clara Everina, dies at one year old. Her remaining child, the beloved William (or "Will-mouse"), dies aged four the following year.

The stepsister Claire has a baby too. Her happy "ten minutes" with Lord Byron leaves her pregnant and "discomposed" for the rest of her life. What's a man supposed to do when these teenagers throw themselves at you, moans Byron. He hates her, but eventually agrees to take charge of the illegitimate baby in exchange for a guarantee of no further maternal contact. The Shelleys go along with it – people are starting to talk. The child is then dumped in a convent, where she dies aged five.

There's confusion around another baby that the group apparently adopts in Naples. She, too, is abandoned, and she also dies. Wait, which dead baby is whose? Keeping up with the spiralling death tally isn't easy. Meanwhile Percy develops a roving eye and is almost certainly having a bit of the other with Claire, as they move from one Italian town to the next.

Holmes follows in their footsteps as they travel on, seeking new horizons and burying children along the way. It gets so grim I can hardly look. The climax comes at their final residence in Italy, Casa Magni. Like the ending of a Jacobean tragedy, the stage is now heaped with corpses, large and small. And when Percy dies at sea, he doesn't go down alone: a friend and a boat boy also perish with him.

The Romantics sought justice, freedom, a new reality. Their "bright silver dream" was "to seek strange truths in undiscovered lands". And in the quest they trampled children and women underfoot.

All my reading life I've been in love with the Romantics. They *are* poetry. They span and encircle the English language all the way from revolutions to daffodils. They have possessed my word-bound existence, my idea of myself. But seeing the rotten, dark underbelly of the Romantic life, I'm appalled. Mary Shelley is living among the collapsing ruination of her mother's life's work. The more I read, the further it unravels. With each small death the light is further betrayed.

During the chapter about Mary Shelley's near-fatal miscarriage, we're in a café near Saint-Germain. Will is asleep, and I'm making one coffee last a very long time. Tears start up in my eyes and I have to tip my head back, slowly blinking so they don't plop out onto the pages. I look straight across into the eyes of a man with a grey moustache who's sitting two tables away drinking a tiny cup of coffee. He doesn't look away: he is neither friendly nor hostile. This moment breaks the spell sufficiently for me to carry on reading without making a spectacle of myself.

Percy is a singular poet – but oh, the selfishness! Maybe not as brutal as his Lordship Byron, but even so… This implacable self-centredness, is it a necessary component of Revolutionary Man? Mary Shelley too has credentials of solid gold, having already written *Frankenstein*. But selfishness doesn't appear to be an option for her, coming of age via a series of lost babies, and forever standing by her faithless, reckless genius hubby. Is it any wonder she gets depressed?

The day this young woman "looked Death in the face" is a horror. Shelley's in her early twenties and already grieving three lost children, when she has a miscarriage. It happens at the dreaded Casa Magni. Percy's account of the event places himself centre stage, trumpeting his own cleverness in having her sit in ice. This does indeed save her. She later writes:

On the 8th of June (I think it was) I was threatened with a miscarriage, and after a week of ill-health on Sunday 16th this took place at eight in the morning. I was so ill that for seven hours I lay nearly lifeless – kept from fainting by brandy, vinegar, eau de Cologne, etc. – at length ice was brought to our solitude – it came before the doctor, so Claire and Jane were afraid of using it, but Shelley overruled them and by an unsparing application of it I was restored. They all thought and so did I that I was about to die.

The word "miscarriage" is strangely oblique. It sounds like some kind of minor hitch – a technical fault on a train. It doesn't carry enough weight, enough fear, pain and death for the way you feel when blood starts streaming from between your legs and you know it's a life pouring away and there's nothing, nothing at all you can do to make it stop. To compound the fear, Shelley knows very well that her own mother's life ended similarly. Wollstonecraft bled slowly away as Shelley came into the world, destroying her own creator.

Coming up from Holmes's pages for another breather, I find that all the fresh streaming hot blood of the Revolution suddenly collects into this one scene. The terror of Mary Shelley, bleeding and weeping on a heap of ice. On top of the immediate danger to her life is the madness of losing yet another child. Two days later Percy complains in a letter to the effect that "the wife just doesn't understand me". This disturbs even the devoted Holmes. While Shelley lies in bed, too depressed to move, there goes Percy, writing poems to someone's wife, fretting about the duality of his soul and larking around in boats.

It's those Romantics. Pioneering and self-regarding, they are the prototype for the 1970s hippy male. Free love and self-expression defines the great poets, even as their children are abandoned or die, and their brilliant but long-suffering women are at best overshadowed. Why do I care? Because they of all people should have known better. Echoes of Professor Belissa come to mind, his scathing disappointment in the English: "They should have been sympathetic. But they were the worst enemies of all, because they betrayed us."

At least with the likes of Edmund Burke MP you know what you're in for. Oak-solid authenticity, like it or not. I can handle that, and respect it in its own way. But no, not this pattern among revolutionary men. Fast forward to hippy kids and communes, and I really start to lose patience. Give me a revolutionary line off some lightweight scrawny-arse long-haired space-cowboy radical who gets his lovin' on the run – and I will spew on his beard and sprint over the nearest brick wall and never look back.

If you really want to be a revolutionary then try not being a dick. A small example, but one that stuck: a friend of my mum's once told me how everyone agreed the contraceptive pill was this amazing new freedom for women. But she saw it also liberated hippy men to pressure her into having sex. If you didn't, you must be an uptight square. Yeah, baby. Freedom isn't just your freedom: it's everyone else's too.

Wollstonecraft knew this. She could've selected anyone from roughly half the population of the world to vent on in her *Vindication*, but it's the radical Jean-Jacques Rousseau who gets the heat. There was no end of fusty old wig-wearers to choose from, calling women whores and bitches for aspiring to be educated or independent. But she picks the fight with freestylin' wonderboy J-J.

Why? Again: he should have known better.

I pull in a shuddering breath and stare defiantly back over at Moustache Man. He's looking at his coffee. I can't calm down – can't stop pulling angry thoughts out of the book, like toxic handkerchiefs from a magician's sleeve. There is indeed a straight line from Percy and his groovy free love to a string of financially struggling single mothers. Like Wordsworth's French girl, Annette. Like Mary Shelley's mum. Like mine.

I'm now clenching the book. Paris is awful, and revolutions are awful. Wollstonecraft is betrayed – and look what happens to her daughter, hanging around with flouncy proto-hippy dads. Moustache Man's still sitting at his table: he gazes around innocently and I want to punch him. What's wrong with me? Put the book down. Drink some water. And finally admit it: there's more than a shred of personal indignation here.

My own father was something of a hippy dad. He looked the part (think off-duty Che) and was big on apocalyptic hippy banter. He was a superb cartoonist. He left when I was small and I will absolutely never not ever admit to not getting over this. He went away and rode motorbikes and ran a pub full of Hell's Angels with names like Tumbleweed and

Zombie. Easy riders don't pay child maintenance, man, and to this day I don't know how my mum made it through. But at least I was an early prodigy in Freak Brothers cartoons.

It took a while to understand my mum's reaction when she found me reading *Zen and the Art of Motorcycle Maintenance*. So do I have a problem with counter-culture hippy dads? Just maybe. Will is starting to wake up, and I'm relieved by the prospect of some distracting company. It's now raining outside. Will stretches, then makes a grunting sound escalating into full-throttle crying. "My baby," I murmur, lifting him out for a hug. Yes, I need a hug pretty badly right now. But Will definitely does not want a hug. I quickly ask for the bill before he decides to head-butt me and trash the joint.

Mr Moustache is long gone, and I don't blame him. Who wants to sit opposite a tooth-grinding madwoman silently arguing with a book? I stand up, and like a many-armed deity I simultaneously scoop the angry boy onto my hip, put Richard Holmes into my bag, pay the bill and steer the buggy out the door.

Will and I embark on a meandering afternoon of rain-avoidance, and it's surprisingly good. Especially the Jardin des Plantes. The monkeys in the small zoo jump about shouting, and Will laughs his head off. But I can't shake the stubborn darkness. I feel sick, sick of everything. One of the monkeys catches my eye and I look back. It's one of those worrisome zoo moments when you realize they can actually see and probably judge you. Little do you know, I silently warn it: you do all that evolving and there's still no bloody point. You'll have an iPhone but you'll feel dead inside.

Heading back, we share several Nutella crêpes and I have a beer. "If this isn't happiness, then what is?" I ask Will, and he grins back at me with chocolaty teeth. But all the while I'm treading shallow water, just waiting to get back down to the depths again. Later that night, in the onion-fragranced room that we call home, I take a heavy breath and return to the books.

Who betrayed the light? Where does the hope go, in these furious backlashes? Holmes says Wollstonecraft remains loyal to France. But her own writing on France's Revolution compares it frequently and unfavourably to another, earlier one. One that didn't drown in blood or usher in a dictatorial warmonger. Just her voice gives me the lift that I've needed all day – perhaps all week – and I can't help but smile as I read that

> *It has been a common remark of moralists that we are the least acquainted with our own characters. This has been literally the case with the French: for certainly no people stand in such great need of a check.*

And who better to give them one? Stand by for a vintage shot of Wollstonecraft Special Blend Overproof Scorn:

> *The occasions of remarking that Frenchmen are the vainest men living often occur, and here it must be insisted on, for no sooner had they taken possession of certain philosophical truths ... [than they persuaded] themselves that the world was indebted to them for the discovery...*

When in actual fact,

> *they had the example of the Thirteen States of America be-*
> *fore them, from which they had drawn what little practical*
> *knowledge of liberty they possessed.*

Wollstonecraft sees Anglo-Americans as "another race of beings" – and perhaps it's this that helps her to remain positive. Despite the fact that she has more reason than most to indulge bitterness and despair, she resists. And even though she reckons Europe will remain, "for some years to come, in a state of anarchy" she still believes that "every poison has its antidote" – and that "people are essentially good".

Her book is read and quoted by none other than the future president of the United States, John Adams. He observes: "She seems to have half a mind to be an English woman – yet more inclined to be an American." And he's spot on: Wollstonecraft does in fact nurture plans to live in America. She writes to her sisters, when things are still on the cards with Imlay, of their future life there. And America is ready and waiting for her. Adams responds warmly to her admiration with the lines: "I thank you, Miss W, may we long enjoy your esteem".

Wollstonecraft never makes it to the States, but this is the dream. So while I can't follow "Miss W" herself, perhaps I can pursue this esteem of hers – her plans, her lost future? The same is true of the Romantics – they also gazed westwards. The beginning of a new trail is emerging. This is not the silver trail: it's the trail of where Wollstonecraft's legacy ends up. With the children of the Revolution. I look at the sleeping shape of Will and hear his quiet breath. Go west, young man.

The next stop has to be the sweet land of liberty, the birthplace of Holmes's flower-power radicals. I may have been born into it, and have the small matter of that father-shaped axe to grind, but I've got questions for the rest of the hippy movement too. This is where Second Wave Feminism began. Why did the Seventies' feminists like Germaine Greer trash motherhood – was that completely necessary?

How did feminism become a toxic label?

Who betrayed that light?

Will, pack your tie-dye cloth nappies, sonny. We're goin' to San Francisco.

Chapter Twelve

Enter the Dragon of the Crock

I'd love to allow the impression that Will and I constantly bump into extraordinary people by accident. But it takes months of setting up – in between, of course, the rest of normal life. This time around it's gone something like this. I ask everyone I know if they know any 1970s activisty people in California. My email ("Wollstonecraft fan exploring her legacy while travelling with a baby") gets forwarded around, and I get lots of replies from women I don't know. They recommend other women. And I keep on explaining and chasing up, and so it goes on.

Many of the responses are supportive; one is a shining beacon. Jean Hegland is an author – her books even get made into films (all creative genres secretly envy each other's lives). We met a few years ago in London, and kept bumping into each other on Hampstead Heath. Once, one of my kids showed Jean a conker she'd found. Jean said "Wow", and they discussed the conker for ages. I was pleased, but also secretly annoyed. There's never time to look at every leaf and beetle and chewed-in-half tennis ball that the kids poke in my face, demanding "Look! Look!" I want to, I really do, but somehow I always shout: "No, put it down, NOW!"

Despite the conker incident we hit it off and end up email-ing each other. One day of deepest exasperation, I send a few ragged lines wondering how she managed motherhood and writing. Her reply:

"You ask how mothers manage to write, and frankly I still don't know. Even now it's hard, and writing with a houseful of little ones seems nearly impossible in retrospect, and yet at the time it was just so necessary. I felt I could be a good mother, wife, etc. if I could only get my little crumbs of writing time every day. Writing fed that part of my soul I needed to keep alive to feed everyone else... But I still believe it's worth all the work. I even think it's good for our kids, to see their mothers committed to work they love."

These dear words arrived on a day when I least felt that things were possible. Jean stuck me to it. And now here we are, California-bound. Other recipients of the email pass my message on or get back with further questions and suggestions; onwards and upwards. Until I hit a spiky roadblock – worse than no reply – a person who says:

"Oh, that. The whole working-mother debate is a crock of shit. Women of colour have been doing it for generations."

What? This sends me into a tailspin. Into a crock, even. I've been planning to trace the Wollstonecraft legacy forwards in time, rolling my sleeves up to face down the hairy male oppres-sors and training my indignant sights on the 1970s. I wasn't prepared for the fracturing of the movement that's happened since then. From out of nowhere a low sliding tackle from *other women*. But then, what if it's true? What if it is just a crock? I slump in my chair and sulk.

It's the elephant again. The one who came and sat in the middle of the room in Norway, when Mayor Knut talked about the life of Wollstonecraft's maid, Marguerite. I didn't acknowledge its presence once while we were in Paris. Hello again, Elephant of Privilege. You shall henceforth be known as the Crock. For a couple of days there's a gentle hissing noise as my motivation sinks like an aged balloon.

Wollstonecraft says: "I plead for my sex, not for myself." Can I truthfully say the same? Who is feminism for? It goes back to the showgirls' dressing room. Those dancers were shoved around, self-starved and mistreated. But not only did they not like feminism, they were actively hostile to the very idea. So who is it for? Is the debate just the worthiness playground of the privileged? And if so, what can validate it?

Luckily I've got someone to ask who will indulge me in such questions. She's used to it. She's my oldest friend, and we went to the same hellhole of a primary school together. I call her up.

"Lucy, can you be too poor to care about feminism?"

She laughs at me.

"Come and trail me for a day, Bee. Just come and have a look for yourself."

OK then. I buy a return train ticket to Leeds.

Lucy does a job most people don't know exists, in a place where few people ever go. She's an outreach worker for a charity that connects excluded families with government services that they might need but do not know about. Lucy goes out and finds them: walking the streets, alleys and housing blocks, literally cold-calling, in one of Britain's most deprived communities. And I've hopped on a train to come up and join her, to tag along for the day.

If Britain's broken anywhere, it's right here in Holbeck, a notorious Leeds neighbourhood lined with red-brick back-to-backs. Despite my boasted Yorkshire roots, these days I'm basically a poncey Londoner. Scuttling through back alleys around the smashed houses it's embarrassing how foreign it all feels. The Leeds city skyline is glittering there: we're only a six-minute drive from downtown Harvey-Nicks glamour. But the contrast here is stunning. Derelict houses, broken windows, random dogs, no cars.

Most of the doors and lower-ground windows have heavy steel bars in front. Holbeck doesn't have a distinguished history. Even back in 1834 it was crowned "the most crowded, most filthy and unhealthy village in the country". Former residents of note include Hasib Hussain, the youngest of the 2005 London suicide bombers, the one who blew up the bus in Tavistock Square. And this is where Lucy does her beat.

She reaches through the steel bars to knock on a door, saying in a perky Avon-lady voice: "Hi! I'm Lucy from City and Holbeck Children's Centre. We're supporting families with children under five – does this apply to anyone in your household?" It's clearly a line she's repeated a thousand times. We keep knocking. Dogs bark at us. Some houses are empty, some obviously not, but no one answers. A sleepy man looks out, hears Lucy's pitch, says: "No, no ta, you're all right" and shuffles back inside.

"Sometimes they get suspicious and think we're social workers," she tells me, "and we say: 'No! No, *we're* not social workers.' Our job is to read the signs and refer people on: we connect them to the right agencies."

Our next knock is more productive: a cheery Muslim bloke with a long beard opens the door. He has two young girls, he says, and takes some of our leaflets about playgroups. Lucy gives him details of the bus route and opening times. But walking away, she warns: "Don't get excited. Most of the time no one answers. You could spend a whole morning doing this and only make one connection."

When the cold-calling is over, we check in with people that Lucy already knows about. Our first visit is Gloria. She's a single mum from Eritrea with refugee status.

"Hello Lucy!" She says, smiling.

We step inside. Lucy doesn't explain my presence, and I just smile too, as though I'm a useful person here in an official capacity. Gloria has baby twins and rotten window frames. Vigorous black mould flourishes up her walls and curtains. It looks like some kind of prize-winning dark harvest. Curious, I reach out and rub a patch. It comes away easily. "It always come back though," says Gloria, adjusting the towel she has hung over the mould growing next to where her two babies sleep. They are five months old.

Gloria shows us around her house. This is where she's tried to secure her loose kitchen window after being burgled. She's hammered three flimsy planks of wood across the window frame.

"Lucy, I'm so scared they'll come back." she says, and her voice changes. Up until this moment she's had the tired demeanour of someone who's just sat down but can't find the TV remote. Now she starts wiping her eyes. She's crying.

"Every night I sit on the stairs with Emergency Call ready on my phone." I examine the pathetic woodwork job. About as helpful as spaghetti. Any self-respecting burglar would be through it in a trice.

The twins wake up, and Gloria hands one of them to me. Holding a small baby and hearing a weeping mother describe four years with broken windows is too much. I carry the baby to the window and look out, rocking him while my eyes blur over with tears. Thank God I never tried to be a war correspondent or report on famines. I try to muster a more professional aspect while Lucy briskly checks the records of contact with the council and puts in some phone calls. Gloria's windows have apparently been subcontracted out, then subcontracted out by those subcontractors. This goes onto Lucy's "follow up" list.

Gloria and Lucy then do a baby massage session together, and by the end Gloria is playing with the twins on a blanket. "Sun and moon! Sun and moon!" we sing to the babies, and they wriggle around and laugh. Gloria is doing the best she can. I'm pretty sure she just wants us to see that she's doing her best. Isn't that what we all want, after all.

As we leave, though, she grabs Lucy's arm, pleading: "Please, come soon, I have no one, Lucy, please come back!" But we have to leave. Back out on the street afterwards, it feels like we've come up from under water. Gloria's small polite voice is still in my ears. I shake away the thought of that mould clinging on, bright-black and alive.

"Bloody hell, Lucy. How do you deal with it?"

"It took about a year to be able to leave work and not worry about them," she says. "Sometimes they're right up against it. It can be so desperate you want to rush out and buy a pint of milk and some bread, but you can't do that. I just keep my manner professional."

The next visit is even more challenging. On our way there Lucy tells me that this mum has nearly had her baby taken into care, because she was unable to clean up her house. I suppress a snigger – how bad can it be? I think about the state of the floor after my own kids' dinner. We pick our way past tipped-over wheely bins and a burnt-out car. Some of the homes are well cared for, though. Holbeck's back-to-backs may be small, but they once were very pretty houses.

"Here we are."

The front door's open.

"Hello!" calls Lucy, and pushes our way in.

We walk through a crowd of flies – the air makes my throat ache. Piles of stuff crowd inwards around a narrow pathway between the sofa, the TV and the door. It smells like the lower colon of hell. We are dwarfed by towers of fizzy drinks in crates on all sides and mounds of boxes cramming up the walls. I freeze. I'm battling hard to keep my facial features set to neutral.

"Well done!" cheers Lucy. "You've even got the curtains open – it's much nicer."

Sarah is sitting on the sofa with her baby, complaining. Someone reported her to social services. She feels persecuted, and she's sick of being bossed around by family-support workers. She grudgingly acknowledges that one of them did bring her

some fly spray though. I immediately feel the fly spray entering my lungs and poisonously coating my innards. Lucy talks
animatedly about playgroups for the baby, and how it's great
for mums as well as kids. Sarah says she doesn't want to go
out. She's extremely fat and can't walk far.

My heart droops as Lucy reels off the details of Sarah's nearest playgroup. This is hard to process: I'm crashing into my
own prejudices on every side. *Her baby is drinking Diet Coke.*
When we head outside, I try to gulp in some clear thinking with
the fresh air. A Coke-guzzling baby can't be the worst thing I've
seen today, but somehow I can't get over it. Diet Coke too, not
even full fat. My mind scrambles to recalibrate what should
constitute the basic human rights of Sarah's world. My world
has an altar piled high with organic vegetables.

Remaining firmly in knee-jerk territory, I wonder out loud
how come poor people have such big tellies. Lucy frowns and
says being vulnerable has nothing to do with material posses-
sions. But she's far from humourless about her work. She tells
me about her sessions at the children's centre, where parents
learn to discuss sexuality and relationships. There's a special
ice-breaking exercise to tackle awkwardness:

"We get them to write down all the slang words for genitals,
and we stick them up on the walls – it just gets it all out there:
everyone has a laugh, and then we can talk properly. But one
time a council inspector came by." She shakes with laughter.
"He walks through the door, right in between big signs saying
cock and beef curtains…"

We rush to make picking-up time at the nearby primary
school, for some leafleting. The leaflets she hands out could be

on anything from healthy eating to road safety. What doesn't change is Lucy being there, rain or shine. It's drizzling as the parents start arriving at the school gate. Some ignore her, others greet her, one comes up and whispers urgently. She's showing Lucy her black eye: the boyfriend breached his restraining order. Another comes and rages about nursery provision. Lucy has to remember all this so it can be followed up.

The leafleting is a way for Lucy to maintain regular contact with her mums, but they don't all love her. When one mum said she'd punished her kid by washing his mouth with soap, Lucy told the health visitor. "That mum won't go near me now." By now I feel exhausted and out of my depth. There's no way I could do this job: I'm just weakly grateful that there are people out there who can.

We walk quickly back to Lucy's office: she has to finish the follow-up paperwork before collecting her own kids. It's at this point that she drops a bombshell. Lucy was recently told that her tax credits are being cut. Her pre-tax salary is below £18K; without the credits she won't be able to pay for her kids' after-school care. In short, she can't afford to keep doing this job.

She's considering going part-time, but worries: "I'm already fighting to get time to help these families – what will it be like if I go part-time?" There's a pause, and Lucy's voice drops almost to a whisper. "They'll probably think that I'm not bothered, that I don't care about them. I'll still be thinking about them when I'm not working. And I'll just have to get used to that."

The urgency of the question of what Gloria, Sarah and the other mums have got to say about feminism seems to have withered somewhat throughout this day of mould and fly spray and black eyes. But I ask anyway: "Feminism is surely about helping these women, so why is it women like me who are the ones talking about it?"

Lucy looks at me and points out: "They've got quite a lot on their plates, Bee." She adds: "I asked some of the school-dinner ladies about feminism. One of them's a granny, and she goes: 'Well, if you're talking about bra burning, I'll tell you what: if I burn my bra you won't see my wrinkles no more, cos it'll all go south, love.'" Lucy laughs so hard that people look over from the other side of the office.

"But I think the others, especially the younger ones, they haven't got a clue what it means, and they aren't bothered. They'll just say: 'You talk about inequality: at the end of the day it's all about kids and work and getting by. Someone's got to do it, so you do it for yourself.' For them it boils down to just getting by." She pauses. "But I don't even think I'd class myself as a feminist, to be honest: to be a feminist don't you need to read about it and know what it is? Anyway. I'm off to take my bra off so I won't have any wrinkles."

She laughs again, scoops up her bags and gets hurrying. Lucy's got her own kids to worry about on top of other people's. Every day they're dropped at pre-school club early and collected late. "I just want to see them in daylight," she says, as we hug goodbye.

I walk through the light rain back to the station and board the 18.03 from Leeds to London King's Cross. I drink two huge cups of buffet-car tea in a row, then go back for a mini-bottle of red wine and a Snickers. The wooden bars over Gloria's windows keep floating into vision. I have never seen people living like this in my own country. How have I not seen it? Most of the country doesn't see it. It's not only the privileged of London: plenty of ordinary people in Leeds will drive right past the end of Holbeck daily, never once seeing what's inside.

I knock back the last of the wine with the bitter insight that Wollstonecraft's primary motivation, her obsession with usefulness, is far better served by what Lucy is doing than by me prancing around the world admiring my fantastic baby. But at least Lucy is doing it. And even if none of Lucy's mums see her work, the support, the networks, the policies and laws designed to support them – if they don't see any of this as feminism, then it doesn't matter. As long as it's still happening.

The book I brought along for the train journey doesn't help. Wollstonecraft's fictional works are a downer at the best of times. In the novel *Mary* her protagonist witnesses the darkest effects of poverty on women and children, and as a result:

> *She could not write any more; she wished herself far distant from all human society; a thick gloom spread itself over her mind, but did not make her forget the very beings she wished to fly from.*

I will never forget Gloria. As the train pulls back into London, I stare out into the tunnel walls with a guilty feeling of relief, mixed with sadness. My reflection stares back. I look knackered. I feel like... well, like a crock of shit. Wollstonecraft thought and fought for women like Gloria and Sarah, and for their children. But I'm just me, feeling pretty useless right now.

Labouring the point of uselessness to its outermost extremities, the next week I'm at a literary lunch. In West London. I stride into the gleaming white mansion, wearing what I believe to be my most literary-lunch-looking skirt. There's Ottolenghi food, plenty of wine, and several rooms full of people having a splendid old literary time of it. How young they are. Young people are supposed to be occupied these days with mountainous debts and knife crime. Not round here though.

I've come seeking information. Having never been to California before, someone invited me here with the promise of some inside track on the Golden State. Apparently there are two people here who are intimate with the place, in all its radical, alternative glory. Acting like I do this all the time, gulp of wine and notebook at the ready, I sway into the beautiful crowd to find them.

Kala has a feline gaze through 1960s spectacles, and a zip all the way up the back of her skirt. She loves California and says I should *totally* get in touch with some performance artists she knows who do lesbian porn. Between mouthfuls of chargrilled vegetables, she delivers a condensed history of feminism.

"The Suffragettes and getting the vote obviously came first." ("First apart from you," I whisper loyally to Wollstonecraft inside my head.) "Then the Second Wave was in the Seventies: reproductive and labour rights, basically escaping from housewife hell via Women's Lib. And in the Nineties you've got the Third Wave, with sex positivism, racial inclusivity and queer theory." At no point does a vegetable attach itself to her teeth or a blob of pastry fall from her fork. I take lots of notes.

Damian is in the corner of the room towering over a cluster of stylishly dishevelled people. He's tall with a youthful, sur-prised-looking face, cuff-links and excellent shoes. Apparently he is a *salonnière*. Whatever this is, he definitely looks like one. A lot of people want to talk to him. I join the hoverers and wait my turn. When he hears I'm planning to go to California to meet 1970s Second Wave activists, he lights up. "You're going to love it!" He fires off a mouth-watering account of the Grand Sur, San Francisco's Mission District and hipster ice cream at the Bi-Rite Creamery.

In a moment of treachery I briefly imagine Wollstonecraft here among us in her rebellious baggy old clothes, with her heart on her sleeve and her chippy, volatile ways. Does Califor-nia go far beyond her – will I leave her behind? I look around. What world of fabulousness have I entered?

Then Kala and Damian turn to me and politely ask what my book is about.

"Oh. Well, it's – it's kind of just a… bumbling around kind of… bumble." They smile encouragingly at me, willing me to succeed.

"Bumbling is marvellous!" they say. Then, igniting each other's enthusiasm: "Bumbling should definitely be encour-aged as a literary form. Shouldn't it! I mean, just think of Geoff Dyer."

"Who's he?" I ask. "Some kind of legendary bumblemeister?"

"You really must read him. Such a genius. He backs up all of his bumbling with so much insight – just pure, soaring intellect."

I go and get another glass of wine.

Reading stories to my kids, I've always secretly editorialized and changed bits. You have to. The blonde girls should become chestnut-haired heroines, and so on. Then there's the old trick of trying to miss out a few paragraphs here and there. This is definitely allowed if you're really tired or it's something intolerable like Enid Blyton or Thomas the Egg-Faced Twat. Eventually they will notice, though, and hold you to account.

But the Grimm tales have never let us down. I'm biased, having grown up among them. There's a satisfying unity in the rhythms: always three sons and the third is the cleverest, or three daughters and the third is the bravest. The small and lowly shall outwit the big and powerful. There are always three attempts, or three companions, or three animals that transform the traveller's fortunes. One evening, tangled up in some blankets on the sofa, we talk about this.

"Why is it always in threes?" the three girls ask.

"Maybe for suspense? If you won on the first go, it wouldn't be so exciting."

"But it's not fair that the third is always best," adds the second daughter.

"Mummy, you're doing three trips and so there should be a happy ending." says another.

"And what's a happy ending?" I ask.

"Getting married! Having pudding! Killing the dragon! Custard!" they chime.

I start to wonder, and hastily wrap up that evening's story so I can go and think about happy endings. No, not those ones, you perv. The thing is, I'm already happy. With a happy beginning and a happy middle. Happy endings aren't the problem. If there is a dragon to slay, it must be some nuanced kind of beast. Perhaps the kind of feeling that British people describe by using a foreign word because we can't handle it. *Ennui. Saudade. Weltschmertz. Joie de vivre.*

Or more specifically, in my case, a low-level rebellion against some of the realities of motherhood. The tiredness, the repetition, the inevitable laundry – all the pointless and invisible stuff. In a word: domesticity. The Dragon of Domesticity. Who, it turns out, is closely followed by his scaly friend the Dragon of the Crock. The one who says: "Shut your faces, all you women with childcare." I'd happily turn a fire extinguisher on him.

Maybe not slay him, though. Something that has lingered on from Paris is the idea that freedom also means freedom for your enemy. Even fire-breathing enemies. How about me and the dragons exchange a brief Yorkshire nod: "Y'alright?" "Alright." And then we carry on, and go our separate ways. As few battles as possible, and minimal slaying. Oh God – does this make me some kind of closet hippy?

Here ends my Vindication of the Rights of Dragons.

PART THREE

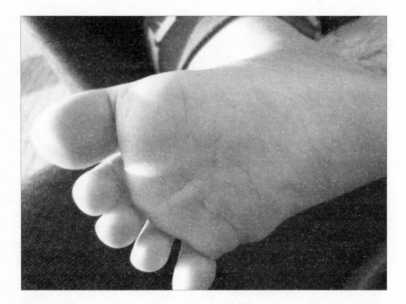

Chapter Thirteen

The Electric Calpol Acid Test

The very long flight is surprisingly OK. The emergency Calpol remains unused, even as the words of certain mummy blogs come echoing back: "Don't ever travel on planes with babies under five." OK, so he does keep running up the aisle, looking back with a huge smile and then bursting through the curtains into First Class, but who among us hasn't dreamt of doing the same? No, he's charming company. And only does a leaky poo right at the end.

We collect our unfeasibly shiny hire car, hoping it will soon acquire some dusty respectability and stop looking so rental. Accommodation-wise the gods of travel are already smiling on me: we're staying with an old friend. Maria Clara was my flatmate back in our student days. She's now married with two young sons and lives in a wooden-fronted Victorian house in the Mission District.

We haven't seen each other since she's had the babies. My mind does a hasty update, in which the entire data bank of a person on her wildest student nights out morphs into someone scolding a toddler in a car seat. As we catch up, I soon get dizzy with tiredness. Maria Clara and her husband Tim say their kids wake them regularly through the night and are worried it'll disturb me. I assure them what a pleasure it is to hear a baby that you don't have to attend to. We go to bed early.

I wake up at six o'clock – *ping* – wide awake. Will is snoring quietly. It's still quite dark. I look around the room, longing to be out on their large terrace looking at the sky. I might even get some reading done, if I tiptoe. So I ease myself out of bed onto the wooden floor, grope around for my jeans and T-shirt, slowly lift my bag and creep from the room. It's lighter in the hallway, and I gently, so gently, pull the door shut behind me. I hold the handle tight and keep it twisted until the last second, fractionally pulling the door until a final gentle click shuts it. Phew. I creep down the hallway into the living room.

It's silent. I tread on a musical plastic toy and scramble to the off button just as it bursts into tinny song. Silence again. I move timidly through the living room and let myself out onto the terrace. It looks down into neighbours' gardens, and next door has a tree full of oranges. Oranges! YES – I'm properly in California. Large waxy flowers on trees, desert-looking plants. It's a Sunday, and the sun isn't up yet, but pink lights up the sky. I stretch triumphantly and bring out the book.

Here in the birthplace of the Summer of Love, the crucible of radical politics as we know it, my guiding star should be Wollstonecraft's politics, not her private life. My state of infatuation has tempted me to keep looking for inner glances, rather than "the power of generalizing ideas". So it's time for a few edifying bites of the *Vindication*. At the time of writing, obviously women couldn't vote, but neither could they own property, enter a legal contract or have any say over their children. This is the case even for married women. For the unmarried ones – well, good luck.

On top of addressing these rampant miseries, Wollstonecraft often raises her focus to wider horizons, ones that remain sourly familiar today, like self-perception and body image. The answers, as always, are *education* and *independence*. Once again her target is idle posh women:

> *Ah! Why do women – I write with affectionate solicitude – condescend to receive a degree of attention and respect from strangers different from that reciprocation of civility which the dictates of humanity and the politeness of civilization authorize between man and man? And why do they not discover, when "in the noon of beauty's power", that they are treated like queens only to be deluded by hollow respect, till they are led to resign, or not assume, their natural prerogatives?*
>
> *Confined, then, in cages like the feathered race, they have nothing to do but plume themselves and stalk with mock majesty from perch to perch. It is true they are provided with food and raiment, for which they neither toil nor spin, but health, liberty and virtue are given in exchange.*
>
> *But where, amongst mankind, has been found sufficient strength of mind to enable a being to resign these adventitious prerogatives – one who, rising with the calm dignity of reason over opinion, dared to be proud of the privileges inherent in men?*

Ouch. When she proclaims "It is time to effect a revolution in female manners" she sure isn't talking about sending thank-you letters. Just as women are ranked slightly above animals and below men, men find themselves above women but below "the bloated monster" – the King. All this must go, she insists:

> *Educated in slavish dependence, and enervated by luxury and sloth, where shall we find men who will stand forth to assert the rights of man, or claim the privilege of moral beings, who should have but one road to excellence? Slavery to monarchs and ministers, which the world will be long in freeing itself from, and whose deadly grasp stops the progress of the human mind, is not yet abolished.*

It's her plea for common humanity, an end to what Blake calls the "mind-forg'd manacles". No one calls all this "human rights" back then, but it's where she is heading. Sadly, though, as I read, I can hear that end-of-advert disclaimer popping into my mind: "Share prices can go down as well as up". Human beings can go backwards as well as forwards. I'd hate Wollstonecraft to see what a lot of teenagers watch on their phones. Technology has evolved quicker than us tardy humans. How are young people meant to process easy access to extreme porn?

And while I'm at it, what about abortion rights? Perhaps the ultimate gain of the Seventies' activists: safeguarding women's control of their own bodies. But they're under renewed attack here in the US, and all round the world. I have witnessed those campaigners outside abortion clinics in the UK. They are the stinking face of the dark ages, lurching anew from the ancient mud to haunt us again. How lucky am I not to have negotiated that swamp to get an abortion? Why should today's teenage girls have it so much harder than me?

Wollstonecraft never once admits the possibility of things going backwards. It's not in her DNA. These are issues that she simply could not have anticipated. We've only just arrived in America, aka the future, and already I'm worried that she might not be able to handle it. I look around to shake off the gloom. The sun is now up. The birds have started singing, and from somewhere around there are clinking breakfast sounds. I'm starting to feel a bit peckish.

Suddenly there's another noise. Is it Will? It's Will's voice. He's shouting and crying angrily. I rush back inside and down the hallway to him, I run to the door – it won't open. I twist the handle as a strange feeling soaks through my guts. It's locked. I shake the handle furiously. He's crying, and I've locked him in. I run and knock on Maria Clara and Tim's door. "Sorry – I'm really sorry – I've locked Will in the room, and he's crying." It's not yet seven o'clock on a Sunday morning. They stagger out: they were up in the night with their non-sleeping boys, and now I've woken them again.

"What? I didn't even know that door could lock," says Tim. We rush to the door. Will is now roaring. We rattle and shake and twist and pull the handle. Maria Clara finds several bunches of keys, and we try them all out. We move on to unravelled coat hangers and hairpins. The boys get up, and they try to join in. "*No hay llave?*" one asks. "*Por qué está encerrado?*" Because his mother is an idiot, I say bitterly, an idiot mum who's locked her baby in.

Will goes quiet. At least he's in a cot and can't escape. What about the bedroom window? I ask. It's locked and inaccessible. Tim goes online and starts finding locksmiths. He calls several of them up, but no one's answering at this hour on a Sunday. He calls some of his neighbours and one comes rushing over with a toolbox. I run to answer the door: "Hi! I'm the woman from England who's imprisoned her baby." The neighbour tries his best, but he can't open it. It's a very good lock indeed.

"Don't you know any criminals?" I ask hopefully. They don't. On the other side of the impossible door, Will sings and hums a bit of a tune to himself, and I love him so much. I try to press down the sickness feeling that's rising. "Well, he's not hungry or upset," I say in a perfectly calm voice. "And he's in his cot, so he can't hurt himself in there." Maria Clara gives me a hug, and tells me not to worry.

I burst into tears.

Tim is still calling up locksmiths, leaving messages in his American accent.

"We have a *situation* here, a *locked room* with a *one-year-old* inside."

"He's nineteen months," I whisper, as though that makes it very much better. Tim sounds like CSI San Francisco. In my head the script proceeds: "No, the mother is right here, in fact the mother locked him in… That's right. Yes, she locked him in because she, quote, *wanted to do some thinking*… Yes the mother is now being read her rights."

"What about the fire department?" I ask.

"They could come," says Maria Clara hesitantly. "But if they do, they will smash the door off its hinges." Sounds OK to me,

I think, as Tim calls up yet another locksmith. But this time someone answers. YES. We all look expectantly at him while he describes the "situation". Will hums another tune behind the door. Maria Clara's sweet boys are still poking at the door with toy hammers and plastic fire engines.

"OK… he'll be here in twenty minutes. But it won't be cheap."

We erupt into cheers, and I sit down and dig out all my dollars. A whole heap of them, sitting there ready. I will pay the man anything. I drink a glass of water and try to breathe in a normal way.

But Tim is still online, and he's found a series of YouTube films on how to open a lock using a credit card. A twelve-year-old girl offers a flimsy disclaimer on a phone-filmed piece: "You all shouldn't do this except for in an emergency, OK, but here's how it's done." She wriggles the card, runs it round the doorframe, then pops the lock. Tim asks me for a card, runs it around the inside of the frame, wrestles with the lock, pushes harder, click, pushes again and the door sweeps open.

Everyone screams. I run and sweep Will up out of the cot in a single move and squeeze him hard. I press him into my body. He looks confused and fairly pleased with all the shouting. I kiss him repeatedly and only just manage not to crush him with too much hugging. I'm so grateful that my heart turns into fluid. Tim cancels the locksmith. Will is in my arms. Wonderful Sunday morning, we all agree, and Maria Clara makes *arepas* and coffee.

As a beginning to our Californian adventure, this episode lacks a certain dignity, and I feel we've started off on rather a Mr

Bean footing. Fortunately, our first encounter is to be one of proper social worthiness, and not in any way a "crock of shit". We are heading to the famous San Francisco Women's Building. It's not hard to find. Its huge exterior is covered with dazzling murals, rainbow depictions of heroic women and wombs.

Teresa Mejía runs the place, and she is almost an hour late for our interview, by which time I've used up all my Will-distractions. As she appears, we're in the reception area and he's road-testing a tantrum innovation. He lies on his back making roaring noises while horizontally shuffling himself along with his feet. His scalp goes bright red. I let him do this for a few minutes while we stand around waiting.

Teresa doesn't seem to mind and, unusually, I'm not embarrassed. If a baby can't do the Shuffle of Rage here in the Women's Building, then where? After a while his gaze swivels round and he catches my eye. I smile, and he gives up. I lift him into the buggy and we walk around the Women's Building, while Teresa tells me its story.

"This is the country's first women-owned and operated community centre. It was San Francisco's first shelter for victims of domestic violence. Last year it was the building's hundredth birthday, but we've been here for around thirty years. Everything you see here is what the community asked for. Even during the dot-com boom we've still been able to offer people space to develop their skills. We have a tech lab, and all services are free and bilingual. You can do job programmes or get referrals for housing or legal questions."

Teresa is San Francisco's Lucy. This is usefulness, happening all around. She continues:

"It's all on word of mouth, and everyone knows us. People tend to be from low-income and immigrant backgrounds. Every Monday we have a free food pantry, and that's something you see growing with the economic crisis. We serve around 950 families. We also house organizations around rape and violence against women. We are non-profit, but I don't like the word 'charity', because it's passive. They get something, those who come here – but we get a lot from them too: it's not a passive experience. It's not that we just sit here giving stuff away. In that sense I don't use the word charity."

"What about men – are they allowed in? Look, there's one over there!" I point at a middle-aged man sitting unobtrusively at a screen.

"Yes, of course," she laughs. "They're part of the community, but the focus will always be on women. The people change: there was a time of mostly lesbians, and now it's more a mix including queer and trans. There was a time of more Asians than Latinos – all these things change, but one thing doesn't change: we will always need a Women's Building."

We get into the lift and come out on the third floor. She looks at her watch, she has more pressing concerns than a curious foreign woman with a grumpy child. The interior design is curvaceous. She points out oddities of the building: the extraordinary stairway, the giant glowing light fitting in the shape of a vagina. Teresa is a good tour guide, but it's all a bit business-like. I'm hoping she'll get more personal.

"Teresa, what does this place mean to you?"

"Everything. My history is connected to this place. I come from Puerto Rico, and before I came here in the Nineties I was already involved in running women's organizations. I worked with a shelter for battered women."

Without pause she continues in the same tone:

"I lost all my family in a case of domestic violence. My sister's husband killed my sister and my mother and my little nieces. I was twenty years old. And from that moment I made the commitment to work the rest of my life in issues of women."

She's talking from the heart now, her Latino accent animated:

"I came here and didn't speak any English. I didn't want to, because Puerto Rico is a colony of the United States, and I was all 'I won't learn that language!' A friend told me about this place, because I didn't know how to get a job. I came here and I say: 'Oh my God. This is the dream of all of us, in all the world, to have this building. Even now my friends come from Puerto Rico, they say: 'Ay Teresa, we want something like this!''

She started out as the receptionist and today Teresa is the executive director. "I love it here: I am a product of this place. My story is the story of many women that come to the Women's Building."

I thank Teresa for her time, and we leave. We head two blocks over to Mission Dolores Park, and I sit on the grass while Will potters around. The Women's Building was a good starting point for our Californian mission, because it's easy to get a clear sense of what the place is doing. It has that all-important, key Wollstonecraft ingredient: it's useful.

What's much less clear, though, is the onwards journey from here. Like all things that develop and grow, the original call for "JUSTICE for one half of the human race" has also splintered. Parts of it now don't even recognize each other. It has branched into individualistic identity politics, where people say: "I identify as this – I don't identify as that."

The First Wave was simple – votes. The Second and Third Waves added new voices and new layers, making it harder to see a clear path. This may be thanks to the huge gains that have been made since Wollstonecraft's time. I was shocked when someone called my journey a "crock of shit", but perhaps I shouldn't have been. I wander around, baby- and baggage-laden, chasing answers and saying: "But what about me?" – and so does feminism. Have we both lost our focus?

Another Wollstonecraft echo resonating in the Women's Building is that she, like Teresa, shuns the notion of charity, describing it as the "condescending distribution of alms". It's a recurring theme: "It is justice, not charity, that is wanting in this world!" She calls more for people "to act conformably to the rules of justice". The veneer of charity, she points out, makes it possible for us to "do what is called a noble action, give away a large sum... weep at a tragedy" while still "neglecting the foundation of all virtue: justice."

Still percolating away, we wander back down through the Mission District. Its quirky wooden houses recall Norway, but this has added edge. Right on cue, a large group of solemn people cycles past us and on up the hill. They are all stark bollock naked. Each house is painted in crazier colours than the last. I think back to pushing Will up the hill in Tønsberg to the place that Wollstonecraft loved. This place has a similar atmosphere, but somehow it goes beyond wholesomeness.

The hippies' counter-culture gave way to another revolution: a technological one. The creative rebels of Silicon Valley transcended agriculture and automobiles, and founded the most valuable company on earth: Apple. Looking around, San Francisco is the counter-culture gone mainstream. As Norway has its vast oil trust fund, this place too is now awash with money. Money and power: Google, Twitter and Facebook all live just down the road. Does this cushion of wealth encourage more of Wollstonecraft's justice? Or does it just allow people to forget?

Lost in my justice-bothering thoughts, pushing Will's buggy along, we wander into a road crossing and get honked at by a man in a car. I wave charmingly and smile. He angrily honks some more. I stop the next person we meet; he's wearing tight jeans and carrying a dog. I ask:

"Excuse me please, how should I cross the road without making people very cross?" Then to make my question more American, I add: "I'm a bit unsure of my pedestrian rights."

"Oh honey, you sure do have rights," the man squeaks. His road-crossing advice is unlikely, yet pleasing. He assures me that once I've stepped into the road then the priority is mine.

"If you're on it, keep going."

"So if I'm on it, I just keep going?" I repeat uncertainly.

"That's right: if you're on it, keep going."

We laugh and say goodbye. I repeat his mantra, walking to its rhythm – "If I'm on it, keep going", "If I'm on it, keep going" – all the way down the street. I'm on it! Follow the yellow-brick road, my mind sings back. We walk past another dazzling mural, two more men carrying dogs and a house decked out from top to bottom with Christmas baubles. In March.

"Toto," I say to Will. "I've a feeling we're not in Kentish Town any more."

Chapter Fourteen

The Rainbow-Brick Road from Interconnectedness to Juicy Nubs

It has been pointed out, by my nearest and dearest I might add, that I'm an amateur, a shallow-end paddler in Wiki-feminism, and have based my voyage of discovery thus far on a few beloved books, my own life and Grazia magazine. Maybe they have a point. I need an authority, an old-school rad-fem with all the trappings, to raise my consciousness. Someone like Professor Bettina Aptheker at the University of California, Santa Cruz. This woman raises consciousness for a living and has done so for generations of Californians.

I know this because decades ago my student room-mate was an impressive Californian woman called Kellie. She seemed to come from the future. She spoke in a manner now commonplace among Tory MPs. Back then it was breathtakingly exotic: "Dude I'm so stoked, oh my God, it's like totally *awe*some."

One night Kellie took it upon herself to explain, at length, to a room full of Glaswegian boys who were doing their innocent best to get vomitingly drunk, that rape was not about sex but about power. It's this memory that made me track Kellie down all these years later. I wonder if the boys remember it too.

"All of that was thanks to Professor Bettina Aptheker," says Kellie. "She's a legend. You have to meet her. She pretty much *is* the Second Wave: she's been at the heart of it the whole time."

Awesome. Even better, the professor is right here, still doing the same thing, on the same campus. Reading up on the wise and mighty Professor Bettina, something stops me in my tracks. Not the fact that she's on a "most dangerous academics" list. Nothing original there. It's the revelation that her father, a renowned left-wing scholar, sexually abused her throughout her childhood. Like certain male revolutionaries of the Wollstonecraft tribe, this was a person dedicated to the defence of the unrepresented and the vulnerable. "The spectre of the radical dad," I murmur to myself. But this is gone to such dark levels I scarcely know whether and how to raise it with her.

During the planning of our meeting, Professor Bettina could not be more helpful. She replies promptly and sends detailed instructions on reaching the campus and finding parking. It's all going swimmingly. As we drive along, I sing: "Beauty school dropout, go back to Fem-school."

The University of California Santa Cruz is leafy and pleasant, and its campus mascot is a defiantly ugly custard-yellow slug. We make our way to her office. She welcomes us inside – "Call me Bettina!" – and hands a small Piglet toy to Will. She then agrees to come and be interviewed outside in the cold, where Will can romp and play about more freely.

Bettina has a gentle demeanour and an enviable New York accent. She was what they called a red-diaper baby, the child of renowned communists, and was herself a communist for many years. As a teenager she worked for W.E.B. Du Bois, the first black American to become a professor. She was on the defence team for Angela Davis, the Black Panther. Bettina has spent her whole life deep in the struggle. And she doesn't seem to care that I'm just an off-peak day-trip struggle tourist. Will picks us some daisies, then goes off to clean a puddle with his cloth.

"So, what is feminism?"

"OK – I've been teaching a class for a long time now, called 'Introduction to Feminism'. You look it up in the dictionary and it says equality with men. But the question is what does equality mean, because it doesn't mean 'the same as'. It means some kind of comparability. My definition is that women should have at least as much to say as men about the arrangement of human affairs. Period. And I say 'at least', because men have always had more to say, so there's a backlog."

I take a deep breath – might as well get this done at the start:

"And what about those men who say one thing but do another?" Enter my rant on badly-behaved radical men. I stare meaningfully at her. Then add: "I wasn't sure whether to bring it up, but I know this has resonance for you personally…"

Bettina sees what I'm trying to do, and she doesn't mind. Indeed, it's as though she wants to talk about it:

"My father did indeed rage against injustice. And with me, his only child, he could be playful and caring. He taught me about crimes against humanity, even as he committed them. I'm a survivor of childhood sexual abuse at his hands. And when I bore witness to this in my memoir, many left-wing people and radical historians denied that this could have happened."

In the same instant we both look over at Will. He's crouching down with his back to us, arranging some leaves on the ground. I briefly shut my eyes, able to manage only a fraction of what this woman is calmly describing:

"The paradox for anyone revealing incest and child abuse is that the taboo is so strong, and the stereotypes about its 'monstrous' perpetrators so impenetrable, that it actually becomes unspeakable. While these crimes are universally condemned, the evidence is almost always denied."

Bettina looks back to me as she continues:

"I just can't explain the contradictions in my father. But he's not the only one. And this allows us to see how the private is political, and how the personal bears its political weight."

This must indeed be the ultimate example of the personal being political. Meanwhile Will has fallen over and comes to me with a half-hearted cry. I lift him into my lap, finding a strange, deep relief in his physical presence – the weight of him – as Bettina asks: "So you're writing a book – what's it about?"

I pause. "It's about whether feminism and working motherhood are just middle-class preoccupations," I say. But somehow it sounds like a question. Maybe it's my new Californian intonation. She nods reflectively, and there's another pause, so I add that someone told me that this topic is a "crock of shit". And now that Crock is stalking me harder than those mums who sell school-fair raffle tickets.

"I don't agree. The problem is not that this subject is a crock, but that it gets privileged over other issues. I've juggled work and babies, and it was complicated, but is it more complicated for a black woman? Possibly, because she might have fewer resources. But I don't think it's useful to measure degrees of suffering. I don't think any issue that's raised by women is a crock: one needs to widen the view. It's all interconnected. Feminism has to be enmeshed with all the women of the world. And the vast majority of those women are women of colour."

The words of Hannah in Paris suddenly come to mind: the Jacobins getting caught off guard by women and Haitian slaves saying: "Ok, freedom – let's do it!" At the time I didn't make the connection about interconnectedness. So to speak. And then there was the Women's Building: as a white woman I was as rare as that solitary man we pointed out, typing quietly away at the computer.

I've been looking at class; the nanny question. And it's bigger than that. But it seems that even if I'm too ignorant to include race in my questions, race will go right ahead and include itself. Grudging respect, then, to the Crock. I confess my lack of race awareness to Bettina.

"But it's key," she says. "Race is always a factor. Slavery is totally defining for the US. People who have had privilege for a long time don't want to give it up. Race, class and gender, it's all interconnected. Like Bell Hooks says, how can feminism demand that women have equal rights to men, when not all men have equal rights? There's no other way to understand it. If you want to see that interconnectedness in action, then just take a look at disc."

"Disc?"

"Yeah, Dominique Strauss-Kahn – DSK. I taught a lot about this case to my students."

I'm not sure, now I think about it, that even Wollstonecraft saw "interconnectedness in action". Her intro to the *Vindication* is clear: "I pay particular attention to those in the middle class, because they appear to be in the most natural state". I have no idea what she means by this. She savages the most privileged and feels bad about the poorest. But has she, having dragged herself up from being a miserable governess, forgotten what that was like?

It does seem to support the accusation that it's easy to call yourself a feminist if you have status, a career or – dare I say it – a nanny. I struggle to explain my worries to Bettina, who responds:

"The issue is how can we change things, how can we help these" – she makes quote marks with her fingers – "'support-ing women' get to college or university? The point is, wherever we're all stuck in our various places, is it not appropriate that women can have a profession? Yes! Therefore – how can I help others have this too? So it's not to denigrate your position – I'm happy you have a nanny. Why shouldn't you? But you should also be thinking: how can I assist her, or are there immigrant organizations I could help out in return?"

Well, there's a proper answer. I respectfully fold it up and store it away with care. The way to recognize the fortune of having a nanny or a 'supporting woman' is to give her a leg-up and improve her lot. In Norway I asked: "She delivers sanity. How do you thank someone for that?" And this is how. Not by making tacky jokes that she's your "wife". But with support for education, or visa status, or progress to the next stage. Somehow. Even a small chance can make the difference. Just look at the Women's Building, transforming angry young victims into majestic, empowering Teresas.

Will brings Bettina another daisy, and she smiles and looks around for a moment. Some students walk by carrying books and chatting. They wave at her. She looks down at the daisies in her hand for a while, and her face is a little tired. "Each woman has her choice," she says. "What I think is sad is instead of berating a woman for having children, why not help her take care of them?"

Tempting though it is to take full and immediate advantage of this babysitting offer, we gather ourselves and begin to say goodbye. Bettina tells us her favourite place to eat is at the Tres Amigos in Half Moon Bay. We set off to find our way there. Tres Amigos is a workers' canteen right off the highway. It's big and ugly and cheap, and there are no amigos, only solitary workers. They plough, grim-eyed, through huge portions. The food, though, is excellent. "Fill your boots, compañero!" I pass Will more nachos, and my wordless sidekick laughs and rolls his eyes.

The route back to San Francisco is stunning. There's a long stretch of motorway – or should that be freeway – that runs alongside the sea, I mean ocean. I can hardly keep my eyes on the road ahead. The light hits off the giant rollers muscling their way into the shoreline. The sheer width spreads away, with nothing but more and more coast on either side and nothing else out to sea but more sea. It's a complete change from the intricate, baffling coastline of Norway. It is gigantic. Will, we have to stop!

We can't let this go by.

I pull over and park on a nowhere bit of roadside, and the wind is fierce when I pull Will out of his warm car seat. We nearly get lifted from our feet as we make a run for it, over the road to the ocean side, down a few boulders and straight onto the beach. We run on the sand together, pushed and harried along by the wind. Empty coastline reaches away on both sides of us, and the wind blows our breath back in as we laugh in its face.

I see my Will lean right into the wind: he spreads his arms and looks back at me. His belly is poking over his trousers, his thin hair is blown back, revealing the dome of his head. He scampers his funny little boots around on the sand. They scarcely make an impression as he turns in and out of the wind with the immense waves crashing behind. We are both small – we laugh and turn and run around with our arms out. This small shining moment is one I won't lose: it shoots deeply into my heart.

I sweep him up, and we scramble back into the safe stillness of the car. We are bright and wind-scrubbed, breathless and laughing. Why are these moments so rare – and can they be manufactured? Did I really have to come all the way to California in order to see my son laugh on a beach in a way that cuts through to last forever? No. It just came this way. Whether he dies tomorrow or lives way beyond me I will keep this, preserved like a bubble in glass.

I will always be in love with what just happened. He's now sitting in his car seat. I adjust the rear-view mirror and we catch each other's eye. Of course not every moment can be a "Moment". And it doesn't have to be a baby: insert your own loved one or even yourself. But there's a difference: loved ones and ourselves don't move so quickly away, forever turning into something new, not being ever again what they are right now.

There's an entire industry of keepsakes – casts of tiny feet, babies' first-year albums. There's an online torrent of baby photos being "Liked" by colleagues on a tea break. But how do you store that moment when it comes? Do you have to be in the right place or the right mood? This has felt like a luminous moth, choosing to land on me. Stop breathing to hold the moment fast. I can't own it – it will fly. Does it matter that I know it's a moment? Has that saved it?

I remember Vita Sackville-West on moments. She describes writing as "clapping a net over the butterfly of the moment". I can remember that, but somehow not the precise discovery of Will's first tooth. I spent so many years pushing babies on swings in chilly parks with a glazed expression on my face – where did those moments go? Did I even wish them away, without knowing what I was losing? The long blurry days from the first few years of a child's life are as intense as anything can be, yet how entirely they evaporate! While the baby that you held and beheld up close all day every day has since turned into something else.

All lit up with this fierce vague sense of love, we drive along the coast back to San Francisco. It's only as we pass some golfing courses and begin to re-enter the city that I'm jolted back into purpose. For a moment I feel remorseful for skipping so easily away from interconnectedness and DSK. Whee-hee – at the first glimpse of a sparkly view! But then, sparkly views make life better. And California wants me to enjoy it, I can just tell.

As for Will, so far he's been locked in a room and endured some weighty lectures. It's about time we had some sparkly fun. Because why the hell not? Wollstonecraft could've done with a bit more of that herself. And it doesn't get sparklier or more fun than our next stop. Now that we've been introduced to feminism, the personal being political and interconnectedness, we qualify for the next round. We're changing waves from Second to Third. We're going to meet Annie Sprinkle, and she's a Feminist Porn-Activist Radical Sex Educator, and Ecosexual.

How do you get to Annie Sprinkle? She's the one who kept evading me, and in all the weeks of setting up the trip she's the one who seemed least keen and most likely to cancel. But every San Franciscan I've mentioned her to shouts "WOW, Annie Sprinkle!" This tells me we must get to her. And when I finally get through to her on the phone, she is gorgeously ditzy and warm:

"What, remind me who you are again?... From England?... With a baby?... Oh that sounds lovely, sure thing, just come right on over to my house!"

So we do. Walking up a sunny hill towards her house, we see a woman breezing down the road towards us. It must be her. Long skirt, lots of jewellery, tattooed arms, burgundy hair. She smiles and waves. It is her. She is sort of granny-aged, with stunning cheekbones and bright eyes. And a very long cleavage. She gives me an affectionate hug and invites us into her home.

Annie Sprinkle immediately begins offering me things – a coffee? Lunch? Cookies for Will? A drink for Will? Something for Will to play with? I can't get her to settle down: each time we sit down near my recording equipment, she leaps up with another act of hospitality and a constant stream of Oreo cookies:

"Please eat them – I am going on a diet. It's my diet group starting tonight."

Will and I happily oblige. When everyone's eaten and drunk, I start asking questions, but she's still distracted by Will. He keeps laughing and holding things up to her face, with an eager "?" noise. And then she breaks off and starts adoring him. First it was the Shuffle of Rage, and now it's disruption by force of cuteness – I can't win. She tries again:

"OK, I was born in 1954. I was a shy girl, but at age eighteen I ended up in the sex industry, which surprised everyone – both my mum and dad were feminists. My mum's reaction when I started working in a massage parlour as a young hippy? She said: 'That's so degrading to women.' There was no sex-positive feminism at this time. Feminism came along in the late Sixties, and there was all this free love – but then there was the anti-porn movement and... where were we? Oh yeah, the porn industry. It's been my life ever since. And twelve years ago I found Beth – she's my longest-term partner now. She's a professor and an artist, and we collaborate together."

"About that anti-porn movement," I cut in. "What would you say to people who think pornography is degrading or damaging?"

"I'd say that porn is a reflection of our society. Cars are far more damaging to society than porn could ever be. Cars kill so many people. And watching people fucking isn't nearly as damaging as some other things people watch these days. But I do think people could be more educated about porn – most people are very ignorant about it. And if you don't like the porn that's out there, then go make some you do like!"

Up pops Will, chattering into her TV remote. "Oh you're so cute with your phone," she says to him, and they giggle together. "You're a regular little high-tech guy, aren't you? Are you calling people? Are you?"

"So, feminism—" I prompt her.

"Oh, I'm still a feminist. But the word feminist's gotten a really bad name, because there are so many kinds – porn people think it's anti-porn, young straight women think it might be lesbian, while lesbians might feel excluded – and people of colour see it as a white movement."

"And queerness?"

"Everyone is queer. We all are: it's just a bit this way one day and the other way another day. And this is the greatest thing about San Francisco – we have a culture of welcoming all minorities, even straight people!"

Between the laughs I'm beginning to feel slightly agonized, and struggling to get any focus. I scour my notes again. We're sitting in the sun on her terrace, skating all over with our incomplete conversations. Annie reaches down and hugs Will. "You're just too cute! Oh, you must have a blast with four kids. Don't you?" she asks. I describe the madness and magic of four kids in as few words as possible.

"Oh, that's radically traditional," she says. "I call that radically traditional, and I love it. A lot of the porn people are having kids now. But it was too risky back then – you couldn't have a kid. They'd take the baby off you because of your job."

She watches Will as he runs back and forth rearranging her stuff. She notices me noticing. There's a small pause then she begins again:

"Sexuality is like life itself. It's so multifaceted: there's no right and wrong. You know San Francisco is the clitoris of the

United States? Yes it is, and if you go up to Bernal Hill you'll be right there. Beth and I did a ceremony up there and pleasured the planetary clitoris: we got down and rubbed it. We take people on ecosexual walking tours and invite them to enjoy nature. The tours are so much fun, and they're all different. It's all about what turns people on in nature."

She leads me into the room at the back of her house, to a wall chart. Annie points out its divisions: "Ecosexual encounters are divided here into the four elements – fire, water, air, earth. Most people get turned on by water. Standing under water, or straddling the showerhead, getting pummelled – it's totally ecstatic! Try it out – give yourself permission to be ecosexy. Then there's lying on the earth, hugging the earth. People who like racing – you know, motorcycles and speedboats? I think they're into wind: it's a wind fetish, but maybe they don't know it yet."

I briefly envisage Jeremy Clarkson coming out and self-identifying as an ecosexual. The image is immediately regrettable.

All of a sudden Annie livens up. "Come on, let's do it! Shall we do it?" She takes us down some steep stairs to her garden. "OK, I've never done an ecosex walking tour of the backyard, but we ought to give it a go. This should revive me." I lift Will onto my shoulders, and we follow Annie out into her garden. It's small and pleasant, and the late sun is shining in. Annie soon gets on a roll:

"If you think of the earth as a lover, the earth is alive: it's a living and breathing thing. Soil is alive – it's full of life, and trees move just like us, only very slowly. Here, look at this pouting lily: it's like a heart of a penis or giant clitoris, and look at this look at this – pollen, seeds – this is the sex organ of the plant, don't you just want to – oh my God – it smells, now you have to inhale deeply and you can lick it – you can suck this – look at the colour, that yellow penetrates your eye: it's giving intercourse to your eyes!"

She really does revive. More and more.

"You should always ask permission: hello flower – we want to ask the flower, how do we know – but I think this flower loves being admired... feel this... stroke this... go like this: it's like the most beautiful penis – it's so sensuous."

We're caressing a lily, then some rocks, then a tree. Annie humps and writhes against the tree.

"Ecosex is all about the senses: tasting, smelling, touching and listening. Making love in nature is the obvious thing, but try to imagine it as though you're part of the earth."

Will and I both follow her as she shoots off round the garden squeezing things, licking things, pushing fingers into soil, rubbing leaves.

"Look at that orange – look at that orange with the green – oh my Goddess! I don't know anything about gardening, but here are some things we can taste."

She pulls out some chives and we nibble.

"But wait—" she commands. "We could just eat it... or you can let it come... come into your body, erotically, roll it in your mouth and let it melt, inhale deeply, feeling it wanting to feed you – and when you die you will feed it back. It's a conversation: you use your fantasy – it's using your fantasy muscles and the five senses of your body."

She then takes the leaves out of her mouth and spreads them out, semi-chewed, onto her face. "It's full of life, and now I'm borrowing its skin!"

"Oops – I think I ate mine too quickly—" I gulp. "Should I have played with it a bit more?"

"What you put in is what you get out!" she says coquettishly. She gets down and strokes the grass, running her fingers through it. "When I was a little girl I'd eat the roses, and my mum would go crazy. Also smelling burning wood and feeling heat off the campfire, all those things are so good... I'm just learning all this, figuring it out. That's why on these ecosex walking tours I always learn something new. As a teen I did a lot of psychedelics, and had intense connections with nature. It was the '60s, you know – everyone did it."

This is somewhat beyond the 1960s, though. She's taking tree-hugging to a new level. "Do you want to be hugged?" she asks a cherry tree as she begins mounting it. "I love you. You're so BIG. We can put our bodies together. Look at it: look at the joins between the branches – that looks like a vagina – you might find a little anus: it's silvery smooth. If you're into penises – and I like penises – you can see this as a big hard phallus. They're so alive – we forget that we take nature so much for granted. Look at the colour of this flower: it's like the inside of the vagina, and it's so soft..." She puts on her glasses for a closer look. Will comes and puts his face to the flowers too. With each new flower and leaf she shows, he laughs with his mouth wide open. It's his open-headed smile, like a muppet. And there's no stopping Annie now.

"This is our corpse flower," she says. "The Victorians thought these flowers were too erotic to look at. And when it bloomed it stank of flesh: it was too much for them; it was considered too arousing. Look at all these blushing flowers, and these juicy nubs."

We go back onto Annie's terrace. "OK, so if you open yourself up and you bend your knees, you can breathe it all in…"

I obediently bend my knees and reach my arms upwards, while Will sits on the floor nearby, watching us with an encouraging smile. Annie starts to pant, reaching out her arms as if to embrace the sunshine, and then moans between pants.

"You can get high just breathing in; it's very ecstatic and orgasmic – it's kind of an ecogasm: you feel that energy of the earth coming up, and your energy going out… it's like the earth is having sex all the time – nature is totally in reproductive mode – everywhere there's fucking and reproduction going on – and death and birth and sex everywhere. It's everywhere…"

I clear my throat and breathe as loudly as possible. We are reaching peak Annie-mation. She pants more, slower and deeper, and lets out small screams:

"So, it's like saying yes… YES… YES! I'm feeling the electricity of the life force. That's ecosex: letting that into your body. Giving it out and bringing it in… It's feminism, but it's for everything, not just women or men, it's all about loving the universe more – I don't know – I haven't figured it all out yet." She releases her arms back down and shakes her hair. "But the best is yet to come!"

She sighs, smiling. I laugh: "Annie, I came here to argue with the Second Wave, and I end up being seduced by the Third Wave."

"Oh, I love waves." She doesn't miss a beat. "You know you can be butt-fucked by the ocean? It's so great, you get down in the water and stick up your behind like this – and it's just the size. Size really matters, when it comes to waves. And the waves come up and slap you and push you and roll you around..."

As she talks I'm thinking that Annie Sprinkle is everything that any kind of activist movement needs: she is funny and sexy. The ditz, the orgasmic display – and throughout the whole show Annie appears to be completely unselfconscious. I can't help but wonder if she's aware what irresistible PR this is. Is it all for real?

But then there's nothing less phony than the next thing Annie says. I tease her gently about finishing off the cookies before she starts the dieting class tonight. She pauses, and in a more detached, dreamy voice, she muses:

"You know what, I've done all the taboos. But there's still one big taboo left. Way more than prostitution, porn, fisting, golden showers or my Public Cervix Announcement. Masturbation rituals, sex in the dirt with Beth: I've done all of that – but the biggest taboo is this: you can't be chubby or old." She looks down. "I'm just a chubby old woman. And that is society's greatest taboo, if you're a woman. This is what you are not allowed to be. I know this is true, because when I was young and I saw fat or old women I was very judgemental. I can show my pussy to forty thousand people, but I'm ashamed of my belly. I have shame about my belly. I try not to be ashamed, but I am."

She is for real.

Chapter Fifteen

The Unopened Chapter of Death

Will and I finally take our leave of the real Annie Sprinkle, hug goodbye and set off. We walk a long way to let it all soak in, to let the glowing magic last. Up the hill we roam, and all the way back down. I smile knowingly at a couple of perfectly innocent trees. But eventually the walking brings us back to earth; back down to the concrete pavement. And as the day fades, a shadow enters my mind. Annie Sprinkle may well be an ambassador for tolerance and fun, but what about the other end of the scale?

We've had sexy frolics in Annie's pouting, glowing garden, but the shadow slowly falling over us is the returning thought of people in a less enlightened place. Not everyone gets to live in San Francisco or Norway. My day with Lucy and her mums comes to mind; Gloria's mouldy walls and the bitter hopelessness of that train ride home. Ecosexuality is riotous excellence, but how and where can it connect to Gloria? Will it be useful to people like her any time soon?

We spot a small diner and go inside. It's pretty hard work having an ecogasm, and I'm starving. I've always longed to order "eggs over easy", and I confidently do so, despite not knowing what it means. When the food arrives, Will's order beats mine hands down. We gasp – I'm jealous. Right before Will's wide eyes is a pancake mouse face, with chocolate eyes and nose, topped with whiskers of crispy bacon. We're still laughing about it, pulling mouse faces and nibbling the bacon whiskers when I hear something frightening, jarring.

It's a nearby woman, and she seems to be crying. There's a small girl with her, who looks around in fear. The woman scrambles to stand up, and it's clear that she's pregnant. She clutches at her abdomen and lets out the same noise. I jump up at the same time that the waiter rushes over. Through the sudden shouting and phone calls, the waiter waves everyone away, placing a protective arm around the woman's back as she cries. A car pulls up outside, and she and the girl get in. The woman's eyes have the shine of terror.

It's over so quickly. The remaining diner customers look at each other and make forlorn remarks about how we hope she's OK and "Oh, that poor little girl". The woman was pregnant, but it didn't look like she was full term. Was she losing the baby? Was that the sound of a death, coming strangled from her mouth? They have gone, and everyone has settled down again. Will carries on eating the bacon whiskers, but I'm not hungry. I lift and circle him in my arms, self-medicating. I smell his pancakey neck and kiss his face too many times.

After we leave, the subsequent hours are filled with growing shame at my lack of usefulness. What if she's too poor for hospital? What if she's not legal and can't get medical help? Why didn't I try to get her name? The sounds she made echo on in my ears, and when Will is in his cot asleep, the thoughts roam wider. That animal cry of pain reverberates on, and I wish with all my heart that I could find her. The procession of humanity condenses in such sounds. Even here in Silicon Valley, the very pinnacle of development, a woman is still in mortal danger on the whim of nature.

I see Mary Shelley, sitting on a pile of ice as she bleeds, and then Wollstonecraft herself, in her own closing chapter. Suddenly, crashing in on me like a bursting dam, is the scene from Godwin's biography that I half-read years ago. I fled the pages, distraught, and have never once dared to return. Even though it's right here with me always, because his biography is the second half of my treasured edition of *Letters from Norway*. It's the scene of the death of Mary Wollstonecraft.

Can I bear it? It's not only that I'm being a chicken – although that's certainly a factor. It's that the whole effort, the point and the meaning of all this travelling and writing – it has all been about bringing her to life. Resurrecting her. So at what point must I look deep into her slow and untimely annihilation? What possible good can it bring? Can't I pretend it didn't happen and only stay in the warm places, the vivid moments, the true sound of her living voice?

I know there is no good in it, but despite myself I look anyway. Holding the book, my dearest old battered book with the smooth and neglected death section, unwanted, close to the end, I turn to these dreaded back pages, brace myself and look inside. The spine isn't even cracked. No aging notes, scraps or bookmarks fall out of this part. The text itself appears smaller, and the language more dusty since all my supersized Californian capering, but oh, it's good to be back with her. Even here.

Wollstonecraft has done Paris, done Norway, returned to London and been finally rejected by Imlay. She has tried to die once more, continued with her writing and publishing, and embarked on a love affair with the radical philosopher William Godwin. This last is the most golden, but also the shortest episode in her story. Theirs is a "friendship melting into love". Their letters are tender, and the relationship is one of equals.

Godwin is kind: he brings thoughtful gifts to young Frances, and he thinks the world of Wollstonecraft and her "unvanquishable greatness of soul". They become an item, to the dismay of London society. Only when she gets pregnant do they cave in and get married, to protect their unborn child from the social fury their unconventionality provokes. They marry in St Pancras Old Church, where, a few short months later, she will be buried.

The "last fatal scene of her life" cannot be better conveyed than by William Godwin's own words. Neither is his account matched anywhere as a blueprint for how Revolutionary Man can get it so perfectly right, in the ultimate moment of domesticity.

Now heavily pregnant with the author of *Frankenstein*, she "was taken into labour on Wednesday the thirtieth of August". Being Wollstonecraft, she will of course have none of the customary medics and attendant fuss. She only wants a midwife and is cheerfully sending off notes here and there throughout the day, as her pains get stronger.

About two o'clock in the afternoon, she went up to her chamber – never more to descend.

The child was born at twenty minutes after eleven at night. ... I was sitting in a parlour, and it was not until after two o'clock on Thursday morning that I received the alarming intelligence that the placenta was not yet removed, and that the midwife dared not proceed any further, and gave her opinion for calling in a male practitioner. I accordingly went for Dr Poignand, physician and man-midwife to the same hospital, who arrived between three and four hours after the birth of the child. He immediately proceeded to the extraction of the placenta, which he brought away in pieces, till he was satisfied that the whole was removed. In that point however it afterwards appeared that he was mistaken.

The period from the birth of the child till about eight o'clock the next morning was a period full of peril and alarm. The loss of blood was considerable, and produced and almost uninterrupted series of fainting fits. I went to the chamber soon after four in the morning and found her in this state. She told me some time on Thursday that she should have died the preceding night, but that she was determined not to leave me ...

What had passed however in the night between Wednesday and Thursday had so far alarmed me that I did not quit the house, and scarcely the chamber, during the following day. But my alarms wore off as time advanced. Appearances were more favourable than the exhausted state of the patient would almost have permitted me to expect ...

Saturday was a day less auspicious than Friday, but not absolutely alarming.

Sunday, the third of September, I now regard as the day that finally decided on the fate of the object dearest to my heart that the universe contained. Encouraged by what I considered as the progress of her recovery, I accompanied a friend in the morning in several calls, one of them as far as Kensington, and did not return till dinner time. On my return, I found a degree of anxiety in every face, and was told that she had had a sort of shivering fit and had expressed some anxiety at the length of my absence... I felt a pang at having been so long and so unseasonably absent, and determined that I would not repeat the fault.

In the evening she had a second shivering fit, the symptoms of which were in the highest degree alarming. Every muscle of the body trembled, the teeth chattered, and the bed shook under her. This continued probably for five minutes.

And so it continues. On Monday they call more doctors in. On Tuesday they discuss operating.

Wednesday was to me the day of greatest torture in the melancholy series. It was now decided that the only chance of supporting her through what she had to suffer was by supplying her rather freely with wine...

...About ten o'clock on Thursday evening, Mr Carlisle told us to prepare ourselves, for we had reason to expect the fatal event every moment... She did not die on Thursday night.

Good God, how long – how long can this carry on?

She was affectionate and compliant to the last. I observed on Friday and Saturday nights that, whenever her attendants commended her to sleep, she discovered her willingness to yield, by breathing, perhaps for the space of a minute, in the manner of a person that sleeps, though the effort, from the state of her disorder, usually proved ineffectual...

... On Saturday morning, I talked to her for a good while of the two children. In conformity with Mr Carlisle's maxim of not impressing the idea of death, I was obliged to manage my expressions. I therefore affected to proceed wholly upon the ground of her having been very ill, and that it would be some time before she could expect to be well, wishing her to tell me anything that she would choose to have done respecting the children, as they would now be principally under my care. After having repeated this idea to her in a great variety of forms, she at length said, with a significant tone of voice: "I know what you are thinking of," but added that she had nothing to communicate to me upon the subject...

At six o'clock on Sunday morning, September the tenth, Mr Carlisle called me from my bed to which I had retired at one, in conformity to my request, that I might not be left to receive all at once the intelligence that she was no more. She expired at twenty minutes before eight...

This light was lent to me for a very short period, and is now extinguished for ever!

In his diary that night, shattered Godwin writes only the words "twenty minutes before eight", followed by three straight lines of his pen.

Still grieving, Godwin begins writing the biography that will unleash a storm. In a bitter twist, he will be accused of causing another death: that of her reputation. The world is not ready for her experimental life – the affairs, the illegitimate pregnancies.

Enemies pick over his work with howling glee: proof irrefutable that she was a whore and a bitch. Former friends back away, shaking their heads. Onto the historical scrapheap she is thrown. It took her ten days to die – the death of her reputation was more effective. And *this* is why Mary Wollstonecraft isn't as famous as she should be.

Godwin's account of her doomed fight for life is agony. The tears keep on flooding my eyes. Doctors have messily introduced the fatal infection with the attempted placenta removal, and I can scarcely stand the part where they apply puppies to her breasts to reduce the engorgement. What the *fuck*. She's trying her best to live. We lost one of the greatest women – we lost her young, and for no reason at all. The unnecessary, lingering loss is more enraging than if she'd slipped and fallen down a hole. It is a trivial, preventable, commonplace and utterly stupid death. She dies a *woman's death*.

Something I share with Wollstonecraft, and would very much prefer not to, is that I too had a retained placenta after the birth of my second daughter. I've always given the topic a wide berth, not out of squeamishness, but because of the war-correspondent tone that these conversations take. They tend to be less than sisterly:

"I was in labour for twenty hours."

"Twenty hours? I was in labour for three days and had thirty stitches."

"Thirty stitches? My womb fell out."

"Mate, you got off lightly…"

There's quite enough of that placenta banter going round. So suffice to say that two years after the event itself, I'm at a party with helium balloons. Everyone starts inhaling, and squeaking in comedy voices. I too inhale a deep gasp, but suddenly everything flashes straight back to the gas and air used in labour. I can taste and smell that moment, and immediately feel my imminent and certain death.

Everything shuts down. I'm unable to breathe or talk. I silently sink down to the floor. I think I'm there for quite some time – it's hard to know. Sooner or later I start breathing again, and then get myself up off the floor, and eventually I become able to talk again. Standing there, confused and smitten with fear. It's pretty freaky, and I wholeheartedly do not recommend it. Where did this come from?

From the manual removal of the placenta. Briefly, then: the birth was just the usual pulsing, primeval madness: wild clawings, donkey noises, you know. The widening pool of blood was strangely hypnotic as it sped across the floor, but it was way too fast for me to register any danger. After all, the baby was out, and she was fine. So surely everything was ok? But suddenly it wasn't. Manual removal of the placenta. In these words is the nightmare. It was the cursed placenta that did me in. Not even the baby – just its lumpen used-up afterbirth.

Manual removal doesn't sound like much. And perhaps there's a way of doing it well. But in this case it involves being punched repeatedly in my already shattered vagina by a male registrar who is shouting: "DO YOU WANT ME TO GET THIS OUT OR NOT? GIVE HER MORE GAS." Followed by stitches, thrombosed haemorrhoids and panic attacks. Followed by years of not telling anyone about it. Not until now anyway.

Of course, I was massively lucky: I survived and my baby survived. And we've thanked god for the NHS an infinite number of times during the having of all these babies. Yet that weird, strangling terror was able to crash into my life at random. The panic attack, or whatever it was, came back to me a couple more times until I had another baby. This baby politely made her entrance in a much more safe and unkilling manner, and that seems to have been the cure.

Wollstonecraft, however, never got another chance. How many women still die in childbirth today? Too many. If it takes you an average five hours to read this book, in the same period of time one hundred and sixty women around the world will have died like this. Each cut down at her toughest moment, each leaving an orphan or devastated family behind. Retained placenta is still life-threatening. Death in childbirth remains widespread.

We lost her all too early, with her unfinished works and projects still in a heap. And her unfinished children, who suffered the loss so much harder than anyone. What else could she have crammed into even just a few years more? Could Mary Wollstonecraft have sustained that hurricane existence over a full lifetime?

We don't even know what we lost.

Here we are, Will and I, in the heart of the world's super-power, nestled among the wealthy techno-future, and a woman screams in raw terror, unsupported in her most basic of human needs. Oh, Wollstonecraft, I never should have taken my eye off you! When I was swanning around that literary lunch back in west London, you felt odd and old-fashioned, and I feared you might recede from view. And sure enough, here among these generous Californian beaches and people, I confess I forgot you a little. While all the time I was standing on the shoulders of your shortened but gigantic life.

Revolutions, France, old Europe – they all feel so far away from here, like a 1940s BBC voice on a crackling wireless. But they are very much closer than I thought. "Good evening. The Olden Days calling here, from London. We regret to report that certain women are bleeding to death in childbirth. However the magnificent men of the future will see to that, just as soon as they've made the flying automobile."

There's a passage in her fictional work *The Wrongs of Woman*. This is the last book that Wollstonecraft wrote and if you dig around, everything is here. The politics of the *Vindication* meets the more personal, inward voice of *Letters from Norway*. In the story a woman is imprisoned, "buried alive" in a lunatic asylum by her husband, who has also taken away her daughter. From her "darkened cell" the woman writes a letter to her child.

She could just as well be writing to the future, to centuries of daughters and great-granddaughters; to me. If it's not too much of a Gothic leap, I like to read it as Wollstonecraft's voice from beyond the grave – as her manifesto and permanent legacy.

She is

... a mother, labouring under a portion of the misery, which the constitution of society seems to have entailed on all her kind[.] It is, my child, my dearest daughter, only such a mother who will dare to break through all restraint to provide for your happiness, to ward off sorrow from your bosom. From my narrative, my dear girl, you may gather the instruction, the counsel, which is meant rather to exercise than influence your mind. Death may snatch me from you before you can weigh my advice or enter into my reasoning. I would then, with fond anxiety, lead you very early in life to form your grand principles of action, to save you from the vain regret of having, through irresolution, let the spring tide of existence pass away, unimproved, unenjoyed. Gain experience – ah, gain it! – while experience is worth having, and acquire sufficient fortitude to pursue your own happiness; it includes your utility, by a direct path... Had I not wasted years in deliberating, after I ceased to doubt, how I ought to have acted – I might now be useful and happy.

Like Wollstonecraft's life, the work ends prematurely. It's unfinished, and we'll never know how she intended to leave it. I hug the book. We've been through so much together that surely it's now time I called her Mary. But finally I realize I never will. It has to be the implacable, irreplaceable, unspellable Wollstonecraft. Woll. Stone. Craft. I've long imagined some future encounter where I overcome my girl-crush, we get on first-name terms and become BFFs. But that's just another treasure trail led astray. That closure will never happen, not even here in California. There are millions of Marys. There is, and will only ever be, one Wollstonecraft.

The next morning I take Will back to the diner. All I want to hear is that someone helped the woman, that she had a baby and they're both safe, that a partner's stroking her hair, that the girl will get to hold her sibling. Please, please. We hover anxiously by the counter in front of a row of intimidating multi-coloured doughnuts. Some are wet-look, some are studded. They are like British doughnuts gone to a specialist nightclub.

It's a different waiter at the diner today. The name badge on her uniform says Soraya. She's small and tired, with a scraped ponytail, gold hoop earrings and mauve lipstick. I ask her about the woman and yesterday's waiter, but Soraya doesn't know. She doesn't even know whose shift it was yesterday: "Sorry ma'am". Today is just another long day at work. The city streams on, and life is quietly hard, and no one can change what happened. Right here is the cruelty of non-fiction. I buy a frosted doughnut that will make me feel even sicker. We leave a huge tip that in no way makes up for yesterday's failings.

And on we go.

Chapter Sixteen

*I've Drunk of These Cups
and I'm Walking away*

Back to the dazzling murals and gracious sweep of the Women's Building. Walking up Eighteenth Street I get a rush of affection when we see the building from afar, with its bonkers rainbow exterior. "Look, Will: we're back again – remember this place?" He runs in the large door, where the Spanish-speaking receptionist and the purposeful buzz welcome us back in. Kids spill out of a *quinceañera* party with music in the main hall, people are queuing for tax-advice sessions and the computer-skills area is bustling. There's even a place to change Will's nappy that doesn't involve public toilets. It's a grounding place, if that's not putting it too Californianly.

It's also a place where I hope I can take my questions forward a generation: we've come to meet Bettina Aptheker's notional granddaughters: the Goddess Grrrls. Tina and Heidi are my generation, just-forties women, running a course for girls. The leaflet has a big love heart and the words "Activate. Enlighten. Empower: A rite of passage training, for girls aged 10 to 13". Tina is a dancer, Heidi is a child psychologist. Tina twists around, moves her hands and perches lightly on a bent-under leg as she speaks.

"I used to work with Planned Parenthood. The doctor I worked with in upstate New York was murdered by anti-abortion campaigners. I'd been there three years, and suddenly we were being trained how to deactivate bombs and deal with anthrax. We were a roomful of health educators, nurses and midwives, with this secret-service guy who's teaching us about bombs. I totally lost it. I returned to dancing, but still wanted to work with health and empowerment for girls. And right here is where that comes together: with Goddess Grrrls!"

Will is pottering round the room, finding small spaces to hide the car keys in. "So is the course a modern-day version of consciousness-raising?" I ask. "A way to introduce girls to feminism?"

"Well, I completely identify as a feminist," says Tina. "But it's been made to look angry and unglamorous. The movement has also had its own changes and challenges. If we called this" – she waves a hand around her – "a Feminism course, then I think the girls and maybe even the parents would be suspicious. This has always been a problem."

"Feminism by stealth – has the label become so toxic?"

"Well, even as it evolves there are new problems," says Heidi. "Take the Third Wave, with things like burlesque and feminist porn. There's a lot of play with exploitation and experimentation. Sometimes this is problematic. I studied with someone who said: 'I'm going to sleep with hundreds of men: this is my feminist performance art.' We were kind of worried about that. But I guess it all comes under the wider umbrella—"

(Will stoops down and lets out a noisy fart. We burst out laughing and lose our thread. Keep your opinions to yourself there, sonny.) This is a tricky one to untangle. For me, the showgirl roots run deep: I enjoy some camp sparkle and a high heel just as much as the next rebellious child of the bare-foot, straggly Seventies. But feminism with tassles? Perhaps the Third Wave has gone to some unexpected places. I resolve to ask Wollstonecraft's advice at the first opportunity.

"So this umbrella – if it keeps on getting wider, that's bound to cause internal problems, isn't it?"

"No," says Tina. "These debates should happen. I'm glad there are places to keep the discourse going. Young people need information, to approach the media critically. And they need to respect their bodies, which is the opposite of the images that inundate them daily. And that's why we're here."

Heidi and Tina have to get their classroom ready before the trainee Goddess Grrrls arrive. But they ask if I'd like to come back and give a short talk about 'Following Your Dreams'. I'm flattered. Training young Goddesses? "I'd love to!" I offer to tell them all about the short but extraordinary life of the great Mary Wollstonecraft, and how you too can hit the road and explore the world, even with a baby. *Especially* with a baby.

While they prepare the room, Will and I head to the nearby Bi-Rite Creamery. It smells of a bygone sugary heaven, has slightly too fashionable deli tiles and is full of thin people eating fat food. We get a large ice cream for Will. That ought to keep him occupied during my goddess lecture. And we scamper back over to the Women's Building, where the girls are sitting ready in a circle. They're a sweet collection of awkward pre-teens, with an air of resignation about what their parents have gone and signed them up for now.

I do my best sizzling hyper-account of Wollstonecraft's life: it needs no sexing up, and I give it both barrels. The time she rushes alone to Portugal to save her best friend – the time she serves France's top diplomat wine in a cracked teacup – the time she forces a ship's captain to rescue some shipwrecked sailors... It's all going brilliantly; look at their faces!

Gradually it dawns on me that the smiles, nudges and gasps of "oh-my-God" and "aww" aren't for me, or even for Wollstonecraft. Behind me, in his buggy, Will has been fashioning himself a large beard and moustache out of ice cream. A brown cascade has dripped all down his front and his legs, and he's beaming. The chocolate varmint is working the crowd like a pro. Wollstonecraft never stood a chance.

Despite the sugar rush and the tide of admiration, Will soon settles down for a nap, and I get time to have a look at the tassle question. So what would Wollstonecraft say to Third Wave feminism? I recall Roberta trying to fabricate a Wollstonecraftian social media response on the subject of the SlutWalks. And how her offer was abruptly declined.

The fact is, Wollstonecraft was a strong believer in the now extremely unfashionable notion of modesty. I'm loath to allow her to appear fusty and out of touch, but you're going to have to trust me here. We've come all this way, so please bear with her now. There's a whole chapter full of modesty in the *Vindication*. It begins:

MODESTY! Sacred offspring of sensibility and reason – true delicacy of mind! May I unblamed presume to investigate thy nature, and trace to its covert the mild charm that mellowing each harsh feature of a character renders what would otherwise only inspire cold admiration lovely! Thou that smoothest the wrinkles of wisdom and softenest the tone of the sublimest virtues till they all melt into humanity – thou that spreadest the ethereal cloud that, surrounding love, heightens every beauty...

Flipping heck, this latter-day L'Oréal advert doesn't half go on. She's really not helping me out here. How, exactly, will smooth-'n'-soft modesty that "spreadest the ethereal cloud" help women get equal pay, for example? Luckily the intro soon calms down and gives way to some sense among the weirdness. Interestingly, she first discusses modesty in relation to men. No less a triumvirate than John Milton, George Washington and Jesus Christ passes the modesty test. This is because they are high achievers, without arrogance or fear.

In fairness, if some of Wollstonecraft's turns of phrase sound so dated as to be barely intelligible, it's worth checking out the voices of some of those around her at the time. Such as the one that appears in her discussion of women being denied access to the study of botany:

What a gross idea of modesty had the writer of the following remark – the lady who asked the question of whether women may be instructed in the modern system of botany consistently with female delicacy!... If she had proposed the question to me, I should certainly have answered: "They cannot." Thus is the fair book of knowledge shut with an everlasting seal!

Were women really blocked from what appears to be an appropriately ladylike field of study? As so often happens with Wollstonecraft, I get drawn further afield by the questions she provokes. Might those poor ladies fall prey to a vagtastic orchid opening wide its provocative throat, and become irredeemably corrupted? Wollstonecraft herself was fully up to speed on developments in natural history, through her hundreds of articles and translations for the *Analytical Review*.

And according to the redoubtable research team at Kew Gardens, botany was indeed "considered to be a feminine pursuit ... popular among British ladies from before 1753, including Queen Charlotte". The first woman formally to name a plant species was Elizabeth Blackwell, who published in 1757 to earn the money to get her husband out of debtors' prison. But then, guess what? Countless women discovered new species only to have them written up and published by male authors.

A certain youngster named Beatrix Potter submitted her research on fungus species to the then Director of Kew, William Turner Thiselton-Dyer. It was rejected, and she was barred from presenting her work. Even though she was ultimately proven right, her theories were credited to a male German scientist. Small wonder that over 97% of the plant species discovered between 1753 and 2013 are named after men. And ultimately botany's loss was children's literature's gain. That'll be *Ms* Tiggy-Winkle, thank you.

Anyway where were we? Back to Wolly and Modesty. She's going full throttle now as she moves on to examine what it means in everyday social interactions.

What can be more disgusting than that impudent dross of gallantry, thought so manly, which makes many men stare insultingly at every female they meet? Can it be termed "respect for the sex"?

Not a fan of ye olde wolf whistle, then. The solution to this kind of behaviour, she says, is to develop "the modest respect of humanity and fellow feeling". While some of the chapter's more outlandish extracts do read like an ancient etiquette guide, its distillation is practical: modesty is a mutual form of respect. This may not be a resoundingly cool or dazzling thing to say. But it's useful. Definitely useful.

When she wrote the *Vindication*, Wollstonecraft had never actually had sex, and she can at times come across as a bit prim and disapproving. Here, though, she freely acknowledges sexual desire:

Women as well as men ought to have the common appetites and passions of their nature: they are only brutal when un-checked by reason – but the obligation to check them is the duty of mankind, not a sexual duty.

By which she means the obligation to be less rampant is on everyone. It's not just down to those wanton young fillies inviting sexual assault by wearing skirts – no. *Everyone.* By the end of the chapter, I'm fairly persuaded by this argument that "modesty must be equally cultivated by both sexes". Even so, by her own admission, "men will probably still insist that woman ought to have more modesty than man".

Still perplexing, though, is the nature of the word itself. It has a doomed edge, a taint of oldness and starch. And pretty much no chance of rehabilitation. Until fairly recently, modesty might have invoked the idea of someone blushing, or perhaps living in a small house. Fair dos. But not any more. Modesty seems to have long departed Wollstonecraft's prized realm of Reason, and taken up exclusive lodgings with religion.

They must be out there, but I haven't yet seen any fully veiled or bewigged women on the streets of San Francisco. But back in London there it is: the regular sight of women draped and covered up. Wollstonecraft deemed modesty equally important for men and women. In which case, full blackout veils are totally fine. As long as the gentlemen use them too, covering up when they're not under the watchful care of a lady chaperone. Just in case, you know.

"OK Will, I think this is it…" We're standing on the street, looking up at a fairly ordinary Mission District house. This is our final San Franciscan encounter. We're here for one last rumble with the Seventies, my native decade and the source of my Second Wave worries. And it's right here, with Deborah. Deborah is a witch, a member of the Reclaiming Coven. The group originated in the Seventies with the merging of paganism and political activism.

From outside, Deborah's house looks like all the others, with its wooden boards and bay windows. I tentatively ring the doorbell, and it takes a while for the door to open. Deborah has an open face, a wide smile and cheekbones, blue eyes and bright-white hair. She's very attractive indeed. She doesn't look at all like a witch, I think, only just hiding my disappointment.

Deborah invites us inside and up some long steep stairs to her home. It's like a pomegranate: ordinary on the outside and bursting inside with jewel colours and sparkly towers of encrusted intricate stuff. Every space has rainbow light flickering in the afternoon sun. Glittering beads hang from chandeliers. Love hearts, tiles, flowers, collages, silk cushions, icons, petals, glitter, joyful kitsch. There's an Elvis altar. And a magnet on her fridge saying "Does my fat ass make my ass look fat?"

But not much evidence of witchcraft. Although admittedly I'm not entirely sure what to look for. Wait, look! Here's her cat. A solemn old feline walks over with a forbidding stare. "This is Mr Tickles," says Deborah adoringly. Rarely have I met someone so inappropriately named. Will shouts for joy and lunges at Mr Tickles, who leaps onto a chair and frowns angrily down. "He might not like the baby," she adds. "In fact he's quite a vengeful cat. If you annoy him, he'll scratch you or urinate on your stuff."

"Nice to meet you Mr Tickles," I say convincingly.

Unlike her cat, Deborah is all sunshine. As well as being a witch, she's an artist and a feminist therapist. And she's giving me and Will a place to stay even though she's never met us before. She hands me a house key, saying: "Just let yourself in and out whenever you please." Another witch will soon be joining us here for dinner. This one's something of a celebrity: a founder of the Reclaiming Coven and a bestselling author. Her name is Starhawk. Deborah reverentially calls her Star. Deborah and I sit and chat for a while as we wait for her to arrive.

Eventually the doorbell rings, and slow steps come up the stairway to Deborah's home. It takes a while. She shouts up a greeting to us as she ascends. We greet her back, and she's still only half way up. I look down and can only see a large dark figure coming up through the shadows. I hear her huffing and pausing for breath. A few more steps, and finally Starhawk emerges into the light.

She is substantial like Deborah, but rounder, with curly grey hair and dark eyes. She and Deborah greet and hug warmly. I hop about nervously in the background then tentatively hug her too. Starhawk does not disappoint on looking like a witch. Perhaps not the wicked witch of the north – certainly not Glinda the good witch – but wise-looking, and a little bit scary.

We order in some Chinese, and I put Will to bed in the travel cot. He promptly falls asleep with his bum sticking up in the air. We sit down, pour out some wine, and I switch on my recording equipment while they catch up on each other's news. Starhawk is running a new programme in San Francisco's poorest neighbourhood: they have six permaculture trainees who grew up in public housing. I have of course read about Starhawk, her decades of political battles, her classes and workshops and activism, and her magic.

"What kind of magic do you do?" I ask breezily, as though I am personally familiar with several kinds. Starhawk just smiles and stares at me. She has a penetrating gaze, and I'm beginning to feel stupid when Deborah kindly enters into the pause with an answer of her own:

"Back in the day, we did a lot of political magic around stopping nuclear power, for those years we did all kinds of political action – and we still do that, and we still train activists."

Starhawk joins in: "In the Eighties our strategy was to get arrested for peace. But now it's more: let's try NOT to get arrested. Well, there are some actions, like the Tar Sands action – but mostly these days we're trying to stay out of jail."

"It's not easy though," says Deborah. "Even today campaigns can get divided. You might get a completely peaceful march, and then someone just goes off."

"Isn't this one of the problems?" I say. "Identity politics is so splintered. It ends up feeling like a kids' party – everyone clamouring around shouting: 'But what about me? What about ME?'"

Starhawk takes a deep breath. "There are millions of different strands within feminism – you can go back in the Appalachians and find people still speaking sixteenth-century English – they spell women with a Y. They won't allow trans women, because they're not womb women! These communities are out there. Also I think for younger women we made enough gains that the oppression became a lot less visible."

"And what about 'Having It All'?" I go on. "Was the unintended consequence that you *had* to have it all and then we all got exhausted and rejected it?"

"I question the term," says Starhawk. "When a woman wants to have a child and a career it's called 'Having It All', but with men it's assumed you will have both. There isn't even a phrase for it. But if you want to see how bad it was before, then just watch *Madmen*."

"That is THE most feminist show," says Deborah. "That's how it was. Secretaries were all sexualized, and working women were fetishized. But in many ways lives are harder now. Even the richest people: I have clients who work for Google and Apple, and they simply never stop working. One told me he had to go on a Google away day: 'It was on work-life balance. Now I have to work an extra day to catch up!' This is the kind of crazy-ass shit that happens."

She goes on: "As a therapist I've had a whole bunch of Seventies mothers who were like: the revolution came first and the kids came last. They weren't kid-focused at all. But their children backlashed and became mothers in the precious hyper-mothering way."

Deborah's words hit home. Germaine Greer once suggested children could just bring themselves up – parenthood as a casual afterthought – and look at us now, making our own kids do homework and violin practice. It's the endless spectacle of the mighty backlash. Where will hyper-mothering take us? Will we end up going full circle? A cat who isn't Mr Tickles jumps up onto the table and tries to sniff our Chinese takeaway. Deborah shouts: "Saturn, you get down from there right now."

We've drunk the right amount of wine, and the feasting is good. It's time to bring out the Crock. I tell them about it, adding "I'm worried I'm only looking at the parts that concern me personally. Shouldn't we try to look at things on behalf of everyone?"

Starhawk perks right up with this. She shifts round in her chair to face me head-on.

"This reminds me of a great moment I once had, with a dear friend." She fixes me with her dark gaze, head slightly on one side, and the room goes quiet. "Going out with my friend Mary, we'd take her little boy to the countryside. There are beer cans everywhere. We're walking in nature, but there's garbage and pollution all around. We see all this and we say: 'The earth is fucked! It's lost, ruined – how can this ever be cleaned up?' Mary turns to me and says – and I never forgot this – she says: 'Well, Star, I can't pick 'em all up, so I pick up the pieces that land right in front of me.' And that's all you can do in life: you just pick up the pieces of trash that land right in your path."

We pause to let this soak in. Something tells me "pick up the garbage right in front of you" wouldn't have been good enough for Wollstonecraft. For her it would have been nothing less than the abolition of all garbage, for ever.

"I can totally relate," says Deborah. "My son, as the child of a Greenpeace activist and a feminist – can you imagine, he'd say: 'Oh, the ocean is dying, everything's bad...'" – it was too much. He once had to write a school project on some tree-saving campaigner person. So he wrote about her, and he added: 'But there was one big problem.'" Deborah pauses, dropping to a deep Hollywood villain voice: "'Global capitalism'." They both rock with laughter. "Right? Like, how do you pick up *that* garbage!"

"OK, but what about the question of privilege," I spoil the fun. "What about all the really suffering people?"

"Oh yeah *that*…" groans Deb. "We used to call it the Olympics of oppression. That is just so unhelpful."

Starhawk puts down her glass. "Oppression is a huge tangled yarn: it's all interconnected, and you really do have to look at your own, otherwise you won't be any use to anyone else. I say again: we should all pick up what's right in front of us."

We pour out more wine, and I can feel the burdens flying off my shoulders. Talking to Starhawk and Deborah is like taking off a rucksack full of old books. I'm feeling beneficent, almost saintly:

"Maybe if one group of complaining people causes changes that help other non-complaining people, then that's good for everyone – showgirls, black women, whoever…" Another glug. "But then it's probably easier to be heard if you're white. Or middle-class."

"That all depends on which group you're working with," says Deb, with a knowing laugh, and she and Starhawk exchange a glance.

Deborah scoops up a mouthful of noodles, chews contentedly and stretches out her arms. "For me, feminism was about telling the truth about my own life. Before feminism, people weren't telling the truth of their lives. But the first part was to acknowledge all that icky shit, right? The rape, and the violence. I was totally part of that wave. No one was talking about it before. That's part of being a feminist activist. It's about keeping going."

"Yeah, if you're on it, keep going!" I add lustily, as though the words of my friendly traffic guru are a rock anthem that everyone knows. The chat moves off into other areas: one of

Star's books is being made into a movie. She mentions her character Maya, "an oppressed revolutionary girlfriend". Aha, one of those!

I jump in and regale them with Gilbert Imlay. I go on to the Romantics and how Mary Shelley too was a revolutionary girlfriend. These guys were just unbelievable… Gathering momentum, I drag in Professor Bettina Aptheker's dad, and even my dad. Is there a pattern, these so-called radical men talking the talk, saying one thing while doing another to their families? Was this the case in your circles?

There's a bit of a pause.

"You want to know the trouble with community?" says Deborah. We look at each other. "People. We're the problem." She repeats: "People are the problem."

I flounder, looking from one witch to the other. I dipped my own childhood into that stream of resentment – this is personal. I'm lost for words as they both continue.

"Yeah, we've dealt with a lot of people."

"Including each other, ha ha ha!"

"We could save the world ten times over, if it wasn't for other people."

"It's true."

Pause.

"People are the biggest problem!"

Bigger pause.

"We agree on that."

They carry on pausing, and I carry on staring in disbelief.

They burst out laughing again and exclaim: "We're just a problem!"

What? I've given them an open goal for slagging off hippy men, and they won't even take a shot. I can't believe it. This is the theme I've nurtured for most of my life. And now I'm right here with the frontline warriors, and they're completely forgiving. The original Second Wave feminists are simply refusing to do the one thing they're most famous for.

I persevere, clinging on to my male-hippy-blaming: "But come on, it must have happened to you? Didn't it? Ever?"

Starhawk looks into me, speaking with a gentle voice. "If you want to grow a garden and you don't want a load of thorns and thistles in it, from the point of view of permaculture you have to prepare the soil and create the conditions that will favour the kinds of things you want. And right now we live in a society that favours the kind of behaviour that is appalling."

Well I certainly wasn't looking for some bloody gardening tips. The two of them carry on chatting away, and I stare down at my tangled noodles. They don't notice that they've made casual mincemeat of my ancient sinewy grievances. I move a chopstick to the other side of my plate and then back again. These women apparently possess the power to laugh problems into complete oblivion. It's horrible. All at once my trusty old indignation feels small, unoriginal, not worth it.

The anger shifts and moves around. It's trying to find a place to land. Saturn is sitting by the doorframe with his tail over his feet, and he catches my eye. What, are you going to lecture me as well, treacherous feline? He blinks. I scowl at him and try to cover up my discomfort with another glug from my glass.

We've nearly finished the wine as I eavesdrop on their internal witch gossip. There's a big Coven meeting coming up in the summer, and one topic is looming large: what will become of the Goddess? Some of the Reclaiming Coven are post-gender, but Deborah and Starhawk love their Goddess: "We fought for her! That was a hard-won victory."

"It's like, feminism's gone so far they don't even want any kind of gender?" says Deborah.

"Yes," says Starhawk. "It reminds me of a big climate-change meeting back in 2008. There were lots of people I didn't know. Twenty-three of the twenty-five representatives in the circle were men, and the twenty-fourth was a transgender person. One young woman in the audience spoke up, saying: 'Look at the gender bias here.' And another person got up and screamed at her: 'How dare you assume to know what anyone's gender is!' We were so flabbergasted it took us most of the meeting to figure out how to respond. Is that a sign of the times or what?"

Gradually recovering from my fit of pique I ask: "And this Coven meeting, it isn't all female then?"

"Whatever female is," they both shout. "How dare you assume?"

And I nearly choke on my chow mein as we all collapse laughing. My face aches from laughter. We sigh, lean back and crack open our fortune cookies. Star's says: "Your life will be prosperous if you use your creativity". Mine says: "Treat yourself to something of quality, you deserve it". Deb's says: "You find beauty in ordinary things, do not lose this ability". We munch.

I check on Will, parked nearby in the travel cot. All our laughter and shouting hasn't shifted him one inch. He's still fast asleep with his bum up in the air. And when I go to bed there's nothing in my head at all. I sink directly into an enchanted deep mound of endless layers of embroidered silk with roses in different colours and lace and velvet and sparkle. It's like being swallowed by a giant flower. I vanish immediately.

At six o'clock the next morning I'm woken by a combination of Will singing and Mr Tickles coming to have a look. I jump out of bed and into my clothes before Mr Tickles can get up to any of his vengeful tricks. I lift Will out and hug him. He's raring to go: his legs are actually running before they reach the floor.

Will sprints at full pelt towards the Elvis altar and starts harassing the King. I peel a mini-Elvis statuette from his fingers, and he runs off and finds some glass beads. He starts hiding them behind cushions. Looking around, I see that every surface is heaped with small glittery dainty fragile things, perching exquisitely. It's not a toddler place to be.

We head into the kitchen and make breakfast: a huge bowl of porridge. It's the taste of home. It's still early and I feel abnormally great. I wander about having a nosy round the kitchen: the *Wizard of Oz* pictures, more trinkets, a stack of Tarot cards. Soon Deborah emerges, just as radiant as last night, despite the early hour. She joins in with our porridge saying: "Oatmeal – delicious."

I ask about her magic, and she smiles. "You've never had any contact with this kind of thing, have you?" I must seem very unmagical.

"No," I admit, "but I like it. Would you do a Tarot reading for me?"

"Sure!" She reaches down the cards and hands them to me. "You have to shuffle them whilst asking them a question, and you need to focus all your energies into that question."

I start to shuffle, and a question immediately jumps into my head. Is there any point to these trips with Will – is there even an answer to the questions I'm asking? *Is there an answer?* I think about energies, and arrange my facial features into an approximation of religious awe.

My energies get hassled by Will dropping something into Mr Tickles's food bowl. I hurry over and retrieve a coin and a teaspoon from among the cat food, then return to my shuffling and energies. Deborah sits down next me. She sets the cards out, making "ooh!" noises as she does. "Aah!"

The cards are beautiful, like illustrations from childhood books. They look as old as fairy tales, as stained-glass images. I'm delighted to spy a queen and an empress in there.

"So, what was your question?" asks Deborah.

"Well, it was... Is there actually an answer to my questions on this journey?"

"OK. That's just beautiful."

The very questions, I remind myself ruefully, that morph every day. But then: this is California, surely I can do better. What would Wollstonecraft ask? In her lines from the gloomy cell, she wishes she could have been "useful and happy". I apply my energies as hard as I can. Somehow the question regroups in the voice of a beauty contestant over a Mariah Carey background: How to be useful and happy?

"Yes, this is beautiful..." murmurs Deborah, spreading the cards out. "The first one you've laid down is the Queen of Swords. She's sitting in her chair with an idea. Your idea, right? So here you are, going after this idea. Then it's crossed by Death, which doesn't mean physical death. Death in the Tarot is about internal transformation. So it could be that the idea you started out with transforms and changes."

It just did, in fact.

"And here at the bottom," she continues, "is a fabulous one for your quest: the Wands. This is about energy: I'm going out to the world and I'm going to find it. And the sky has all the cups – it's like I've learnt, I've drunk of these cups and I'm walking away. But look, they're still full, so it's just saying I've had enough and I'm moving on from this."

I've drunk of these cups and I'm walking away. The sky has all the cups… I've drunk of these cups and I'm walking away. The bottomless dish of coffee, eternally recruiting my spirits. Is this Wollstonecraft?

"Behind this and passing is Justice, and this is a major one. This is some idea of fairness or setting things right. The most important thing is what you see – is there anything you see in it?"

Justice! Justice. That's what we're supposed to drink from Wollstonecraft's dish of coffee? Am I doing this right? I'm trying my best, but it feels a bit like an imaginary shopping game.

"Ermm," I waver. "I'm not sure how to think about that."

"I'm not sure either, but there's some major idea in here," she says reassuringly. "Maybe that was the 'Having It All'? The balance – you're thinking about feminism and all that. Now it's the Swords: time for a retreat and to process all the thoughts.

Oh, wonderful. This is the question right here.. and this is you. This is YOU: the Star is the universal consciousness card – it's being in touch with the earth, world, water and stars. That's great for you, right there and – oh my Goddess – look at this: you have the Empress! The Goddess, right? Fertility. That's a very creative matrix right now."

Who doesn't love stars, fertility and empresses? I'm enjoying all this a bit too much. But for the life of me I can't think of a single thing to say. So I make some pleasure-based noises in my throat instead. Next we glide onwards into the Hopes and Fears aisle.

"These are your major arcana," she says. "These are what matter to you, right now."

"That one's a bit scary."

"What?"

"That funny hand coming out of a cloud."

"Well, it's something being offered – an emotional offering – and you're not ready to take it. You're saying: 'I'm not ready, I don't want to look at that.' So there might be something you're resisting?"

Would that be the Crock? Or Starhawk's permaculture gardening advice? That brief episode in which my sacred and defining issues were fed into a woodchip machine and spread out for mulch? No, I certainly was not ready for that.

I cannot immediately determine whether I ought to rejoice at having turned over in this solitude a new page in the history of my own heart.

Even so, it's all getting me onto something of a mystical high. My rational mind knows that the cards can't be caught out or be made to be wrong. It's not like you ask them to reveal your true love and they reply: "Beware of tracksuit bottoms because your child will pull on them really hard in the checkout queue." But still. There's something in it.

This ancient and mysterious rite makes you try to answer your own questions. The cards make you reflect, and they make you wonder. That has to be a good thing. I reach out and give the Wollstonecrafty Queen of Swords a little pat. My inner stores of universal consciousness are all stocked up like a shelf full of baked beans and Marmite. It's not going to be easy to leave the safe warm world of Deborah. When I grow up, I want to be a witch.

Chapter Seventeen

The Croak

Goodbye, San Francisco, you most magical of places. I scoop
up my Elvis-hassling life-enhancing boy, and we head out to
find the car. Our stuff is heaped around us again, and we're
back on the road. I type the next destination into the Satnav so
she can guide us there with her irksome lady-voice. She reckons
only a couple of hours. It's a clear and sunny day, and I'm full
of that now familiar mix of fear and joy. We're heading to an
unknown place – where will we sleep tonight, what will we
see when we wake up?

We drive out of the heart of San Francisco, "the cool grey
city of love", away from the wooden houses cohabiting with
the steel and concrete skyscrapers. The trip north delivers
us to that handsome beast, the Golden Gate Bridge. Rugged
splendour, sunlight bouncing off its orange Art Deco towers:
how is anyone supposed to be able to drive over it in a straight
line? I fall a little bit in love. Like all good American things it
is nothing less than the triumph of optimism: the bridge they
said could never be built.

We cross over, agog. Over the bridge and northwards into
the mountain lines of the Golden Gate National Park on the
other side. It's not golden, and there's no gate, but there is

a rainbow tunnel. I promise you: an actual rainbow tunnel. "Look Will!" We drive right in.

It is now the last stage of the last journey, and we've been saving Jean up until the end. She's the one I met in London, the one with time to talk about conkers, the one who said: "Yes, mothers can write – indeed they should." Jean Hegland, author of *Still Time*, *Windfalls* and *Into the Forest*, has three kids, Disney-large eyes and a sarcastic streak that's downright un-American. And she lives in fifty-five acres of wooded wildness.

We've arranged to meet in the town of Healdsburg because there's no way Ms Satnav will be able to locate Jean's wilderness home. From there we set off in convoy, and I follow Jean's tail-lights obediently through the gathering darkness. We turn onto a smaller track, then another. This goes on for a long time. It's like following Mr Tumnus. The trees get taller until they touch above us, blocking out the stars. Finally there are lights up ahead and we slow down. I pull in behind her, and we step out into the smell of pine trees and night-time.

The house has a large porch covered in plants. Jean's husband Douglas comes out to greet us. Douglas is a teacher and Shakespeare enthusiast with dashing white hair and a collection of ancient Volvos lounging around the drive. Their wooden house is filled with books, books books books, and a piano. The kitchen has slow-cooked food and different kinds of honey. And proper tea.

There's a cat sitting with its paws folded: it's called Kitty. Another notch on Will's international cat-victim tally: he advances on Kitty's tail. Kitty takes this in his stride. "We're going to like it here," I silently say to Will. I'd love to be a fun and gracious guest, but within about ten minutes Will and I are both in bed, fast asleep.

In the morning the light filters through the greenery, with an underwater quality. Jean takes us out to walk around her forest. The trees are immense. You have to bend your head right the way back to see their tops. We walk along talking, and she introduces us to giant redwoods, native ferns, redwood sorrel, poison ivy, peeling madrone trees and a surprised baby fire salamander underneath a log.

We scramble through dense underbrush along a creek and up steep slopes, lifting Will over fallen branches and round improbably large tree stumps. We soak up the foresty sounds and lose our way. It's miles to the next anything. I'm a bit scared of the wilderness, I tell her. Jean laughs and says it's not wilderness. I laugh back and say: "I'm from England, and this is wilderness."

It feels so far from the world that the passing of time doesn't happen in a straight line. We meander back home and mosey around. At some point we organize and get ready for the following day's activities. Reluctant though I am, we have to emerge from the forest. Jean is giving a reading in the morning, and in the afternoon I've got us tickets to see Eve Ensler's *Vagina Monologues*. On top of all this, it's International Women's Day.

"Let's all go on a consciousness-raising day out!" cheers Jean.

We leave early for her event, at a conference called 'Women on Writing'. Jean is appearing with the African-American poet Camille T. Dungy. Their readings are thoughtful and stately. It's all very elevating. But then there's an open-mic session, and apparently everyone's got something to chip in about women writing. Things all go a bit random and blogospheric. Hark at me with my total lack of dramatic irony. Anyway, about seven or eight women writers in, something disgusting happens.

I've got Will on my lap and I'm stroking the curls of his hair, when my fingers encounter a small, warm lump. Some kind of soft growth. I get a bad gut feeling and lift the hair at the back of his head, peering closer. It's a tick. A live creature is burrowing into my baby's neck. This instantly sickens the world all around me and my throat shrivels. Do I leave it or yank it off? Is it true that their head stays behind and then you die of blood poisoning? I wildly signal to Jean: she comes round and knows exactly what to do. She whips out some tweezers, seizes the parasite and crushes it right there.

The other women writers throng round to see what's wrong with the unhappy and very noisy baby. I'm told to observe him. I'm told he should be fine – as long as he doesn't spike a fever in the next few weeks. I'm told he's most likely OK: these things happen. The first few pieces of advice are welcome – the next few less so, and before long I get the angry, vulnerable feeling of being judged and want to reclaim the tweezers and jab a few well-meaning commentators in the eye.

I've let my poor Will down. A burst of fiery tenderness aches in my chest as he leans his head on me, pushing into me. I enclose the entire, sweet weight of him. I shut my eyes and whisper into his hair that I'm sorry. I reach my arms all the way around him, encircling him with myself, as if trying to protect him retrospectively. It takes a while for the world around us to come back into focus.

Camille the poet is a majestic woman. Apparently she once told Jean that she'd love to write about motherhood and to convey the feelings that she has for her daughter. But she didn't want people to think she was "on the mommy drugs". Her poems are the big questions – death and slavery. She continues with the reading but I'm distracted by the credibility gap of motherhood as subject matter. Just look at movies, where car chases outnumber mothers by a ratio of precisely eighty-two hundred to one. Mommy drugs indeed. I say *inhale*. There are worse drugs out there.

Motherhood is not deemed worthy as book material – or even, let's face it, a job description. I summon two of my wisest friends to mind, both full-time mums. They're clever, brutally funny, and both get in a twist about what to call themselves when they meet new people. "Why can't we big up the subject?" I later ask Jean. "Motherhood is all about reinvention, heaving passions, hard physical labour and going round the bend. Surely that's quite glamorous – there's plenty there to be going on with, isn't there?"

Jean not only agrees: she wrote a novel about it. She goes further than Camille: "Out here in puritan America, where we generally have no trouble bragging, the people who celebrate motherhood are typically neo-conservatives and the Christian right, so any of the rest of us who might have stumbled into motherhood's great pleasures and deeper meanings find ourselves scared of coming off like lobotomized Jesus-wives."

Mommy drugs, lobotomies? Not quite what I had in mind. That's how Stephen King would write Motherhood. What about the good stuff?

We've left the 'Women on Writing' behind, stopped off for burritos, and now it's time for the afternoon's entertainment: collective enlightening with the *Vagina Monologues*. We're hovering around outside the theatre figuring out where to collect our tickets when something catches my eye.

A woman with granny-ish hair and sensible shoes is standing by the door, handbag on her arm, giving out leaflets. She's wearing some kind of inflatable pink suit – it looks like giant rashers of lurid bacon draped over her shoulders – and a small round pink hat. It's somehow familiar – I stare for a moment more. The penny drops and I go over and greet her:

"Hello. Are you a vagina?"

"Why, yes I am!" she crows, patting down her four-foot padded labia and drawing them round herself like a precious shawl. "I'm so glad you could tell – don't you just love it?" She jauntily adjusts the shiny pink hat. "Are you coming to the show?" Her name is Suzette, and she's leafleting for further productions of the *Monologues*. Jean and I both hug Suzette, star-struck, and get Will's photo taken with her. This will be one to bring out when his teenage mates come over to play *Call of Duty Advanced Warfare*.

A couple of haranguing hours later we're in the car, driving back to the forest again. Phew. We're both annoyed, and trying to figure out why.

"I'm glad it exists, and I'm sure it was necessary," I say, "but I can't help feeling patronized. It feels outdated. And not quite mother-lovin' enough for me. Do you think there could be a penis monologues?"

"Come on!" says Jean. "I think they'd argue that Western civilization has been one long penis monologue ever since Aristotle!"

"But I didn't like the scornfulness towards men."

"Yeah, even the guy who loved vaginas was boring and dull and not hot."

Will sings in his little car seat behind us. We both feel a little guilty and unsisterly for not joining in the collective whooping. Are we beyond consciousness-raising?

"I guess I don't want it re-raised," says Jean. "But there's also a lot of stuff missing from the *Vagina Monologues*. What about labioplasty, vajazzling, hymen restoration? What about cross- and post-gender debates? What about trans men and women? And letting men join in? What about dialogues rather than monologues?"

"And what about motherhood?"

"Motherhood is such a layered question: you can't escape that there's one layer to do with culture, and then another biological layer. That's the one thing that took me by storm when I had kids – the sheer physicality. That baby comes out and it's just… oh my God…" She groans with passion. "On the one hand I'd sometimes think: fuck, I wish Douglas would do more dishes, but on the other I was so grateful, because I never had to leave my baby. There were moments when I'd have given my life to have someone show up and say: 'Hey, I'll take the kids for a moment.' But when it really mattered, when I had to travel for work, Douglas would take over. And it was basically my choice: I could have gone back to work much sooner if I'd wanted."

I stare out at the brake lights in a long red chain up ahead of us. "It's like we're free to choose, but those choices are hard, and somehow they make it complicated either way. Because it's not assumed that we'll tie the baby onto our backs and go straight back out to plough the fields. Those women just don't know they're born."

"Oh yes, those lucky girls," says Jean, laughing. "They have it so easy, don't they! But seriously, that's kind of the bottom line, isn't it? This is what kids struggle with nowadays: what will I be when I grow up? Such a weird question. For humans to wonder what they will be, and the idea that you can even choose, is sort of a new thought in the history of the world."

I am the first of a new genus.

Back at Jean's home. Ruby-throated humming birds buzz around her porch door. Some thirsty bees have assembled in a shimmering black heap on a dish of water. Bringing my diverse encounters and questions back here is like having a trying-on session after a blow-out shopping trip. Posing and mincing around, asking Jean what she thinks of my new thigh-high boots or hemp sandals. Actually, that particular brand of identity politics doesn't really fit: you've got a VPL now that you're wearing it outside of the changing room. Too sparkly? How about if we accessorize with a little eighteenth-century Reason – there now, just right!

Jean is pottering in the kitchen, Doug comes in from teaching his classes, Will is bumbling around the cat and Jean's youngest child Garth is here for some dinner. He's twenty and a student. He's tall and skinny, and looks like a model, but without the self-awareness. He's cut his own hair, leaving bald patches round the sides as though he's moulting, and is wearing falling-down jeans and knackered Converse hi-tops.

"So, Garth, you're a young person," I say in the chirpy voice that makes my own kids rolls their eyes. "What do you and your friends think of the term 'feminist'?"

"Feminism is a bit dated, maybe," he says between mouthfuls of Jean's pasta. "I don't really think about gender: we're just people. It's not OK to raise one gender above the other: we need a more androgynous society. I don't think anyone gets a better deal. I can't wear a dress without raising eyebrows."

"And what can't women do without raising eyebrows?" I ask. Long silence. "I don't know."

Jean chimes in from the kitchen area: "Old men are privileged in ways they don't deserve, but I think that young men now are challenged in ways they don't deserve for being male. In some ways it has been overcompensated." She pops right out, a pan in one hand. "But I'm still definitely a feminist."

Doug comes over and sits down next to Will, tenderly helping to spoon in his pasta. "In general, the young women in my classes don't realize who fought for the rights they enjoy and take for granted."

"But should they?" I ask. I'm getting a bit bored of the gratitude argument. "Is feeling thankful really your best reason? The witches told me: 'You don't understand what it was like before, in the 1950s.' And it's true, I don't. But isn't that a good thing?"

"But that's why I get so cross that young women won't call themselves feminists." says Jean, sitting down at the table.

"It's denying an important part of history. It denies Mary Wollstonecraft. It denies the suffragettes, and all the women of the Seventies who did so much for us. That was so urgent and necessary at the time."

Garth joins in. "There's a middle ground, though. You don't have to call yourself a feminist to respect the movement. If you wanted to respect every cause, there are so many things you'd have to call yourself. Like, we shouldn't forget slavery – so does that mean we have to go around calling ourselves abolitionists?"

"People don't have to say they're abolitionists, no, but they shouldn't say I'm NOT an abolitionist," says Jean. "You don't have to be it, but you can't go around dissing it and removing yourself from it."

"In Britain a lot of women won't touch the label with a barge pole," I add.

"Wait, what?" says Garth.

"In Britain lots of women, especially younger—"

"No, I meant the pole thing – what was that?"

"Oh, a barge pole. It's something you keep on board a boat for poking away other boats and the sides of the canal. And it's long."

"That's awesome. We'd say a ten-foot pole in America."

"Well a barge pole is even longer than that," I say with authority. "And that's how much people don't like feminism."

Jean weighs in again: "We need only to ask: 'What's the definition of a feminist?' And I believe it's someone who thinks all genders should have equal responsibilities and equal opportunities."

"Isn't that an 'equalist'?" fires back Garth.

Doug quietly adds: "I think people should have equal but different rights."

"What?" shouts everyone, at once.

"Well, women have babies and men don't – and so to be equal we have to take that into account."

I think I know what he's saying, but it seems to be a slightly heretical position. I meanly keep quiet and let him be pounced on by his own family.

"What are you *talking* about?"

"Do you mean reproductive rights?"

Doug makes a teacherly gesture, hands spread apart, and speaks thoughtfully: "Back in Mary Wollstonecraft's time, women were considered both different and inferior. The philosophical shift that was made was that you could say: 'Yes, something can be different, but not inferior – and being different does not render it devoid of rights.' Discussing literature with my students is how you get to see these ideas roll back and forth, and re-emerge."

There's an empty moment, with only cutlery scratching. Everyone frowns and looks at their food. Will stops eating and looks up, gazing quizzically from person to person. Doug has scored a direct hit on the tension between difference and equality, and I'm secretly enjoying his struggle.

"What about single parents, a single dad?"

"And *human* rights is called that for a reason, you know!"

I look over at Will. As the conversation tips into the familiar back-and-forth, I watch him fumbling around with a bit of stray pasta. He's not a man or woman, just my Will – a small being, becoming whatever he will be, not knowing about inequality or difference. He is happily unaware of interconnectedness, of conflicting oppressions and -isms. What if he were a single parent? Or trans? Would he be helped by Wollstonecraft's call for "JUSTICE for one half of the human race"?

The umbrella will just have to keep growing wider, however scrappy it gets, however defiantly we need our own stories. It's like an oasis, a calm refuge, to look across and see Will sitting there. His head scarcely reaches up to the level of his bowl. He peeps over at me, and we smile. Then, almost immediately he lets out an angry wail. Is that enough pasta? As I move to help him he knocks over his water.

Maybe that's enough everything. Once again, like a dictatorial egg-timer, Will intervenes when things have boiled on for too long: I will start throwing food if you keep banging on about the width of umbrellas. Enough is enough.

Harbin Hot Springs. This place has been on my radar for some time. It's a 5,000-acre spa retreat whose website says: "During your stay you become part of our community." Is that a warning? The place is top of the list of "woo woo" Californian things to do, and is renowned as the home of Watsu, or water-based re-birthing therapy. I check out this practice online and then wish I hadn't. I am not keen on hairy men cradling me and breathing in my face. But "travel", as Wollstonecraft tells us, is "the completion of a liberal education". And when in California...

I phone up to make the reservation, and hear that my Watsu therapist's name is Patty. "What's Patty like?" I ask, ardently wishing not to hear "he's a great guy". Luckily no. "Patty's awesome, she's one of our best."

"OK then book me in," I say, then call out: "Jean, do you want me to book for you as well?"

"No thanks. I can't get water in my ears."

"You sure?"

"Oh yes I'm quite sure."

Harbin is a two-hour drive from Jean's place. We check in and wander around through some basic huts, trying to find the Watsu location. We spot a series of small domes up on the mountainside and, leaving Jean and Will behind, I hurry up there. I approach some small hobbity-looking houses around a steaming pool with a rainbow tepee over the top. A thin, shaggy man with reflective sunglasses waves and says: "Hey. I'm Antelope."

"Hello Antelope."

I do not want to be rebirthed by Antelope. I advance cautiously and look into the pool. There is a smiling woman rising from the water. She has a pretty and sensible face, like a reliable milkmaid – and extremely enormous breasts.

"Hi! You must be Bee!"

"Yes, are you Patty?" I reply to her face. Her face. Talk to her face.

"Why, yes I am – take a shower and come on in!"

Gulp. She's naked. I brought a swimming costume along, but don't want to seem uptight. So I have a quick shower and stride nakedly forth into the warm water as if to say: "Why, I do this every other day."

"OK, it's your first time," says Patty encouragingly. How can she possibly tell.

"Anything you want to tell me about your body?"

"Erm – I don't really think about my body all that much, but I do have four kids, so maybe I'd like to unwind a bit," I say, the tension rising as I imagine being engulfed in her capacious bosoms.

"OK, now let's see how you float," she says, and supporting my head she lightly pulls me along while my body flails awkwardly.

"Oh," she exclaims. "You're going to need a lot of floating support!"

"Do I lack normal flotation skills?"

"No, dear: it's just if you have a lot of energy and movement it can affect how you are in the water."

I'm a special-needs floater. Patty attaches two floats to my legs, one around each shin, and takes my head again. This time I lift up and float into an obedient baby position. I feel like a diagram of an unborn baby at about six months' gestation. My arms and legs are small floating appendages. She begins to rock me from side to side and questions stampede into my mind as I firmly screw my eyes shut.

What if I bump into her breasts? My breasts are intimidated. Is this sexual? I don't want it to be sexual. And what if I need to cough – or scratch my nose? What if she talks or breathes on me, or utters some ecstatic moan and I have an attack of giggles? Can she see my fanny? Is it too Brazilian for this environment? I bet everyone else has bushy fannies. Mine suddenly feels like a traitor. Is Antelope in the water too?

I shut my eyes a fraction less fiercely, and some light gets in through my eyelashes. We are gently moving between sunny patches in the water, and I can just make out the colours of the tepee overhead. I lie back, and my ears go under the water. I can hear some distant bubbling and squeaky noises. It's very amniotic. It makes me think about being a baby.

It's quite powerful, the weightlessness of being in water, and the weightlessness of not being able to see or hear anything. I start to feel like a baby. I sneak a secret peep out of one eye, to make sure Patty's not spying on me, or rolling back her eyes while chanting a Native American incantation. But no: she's gazing peacefully into the distance. That's OK. Eyes closed again.

Soon I start to feel that Patty loves me. My mind tells me this is absurd, but I can just tell she really does. She's doing deep yoga breathing, but not in an impolite way. Just enough so I know she's there. The movements blur and roll, concertina-like, and I lose track of gravity, and of where my swaying spine and legs are. Everything is mildly floating away.

There's a small panic when I think she's passed me on to Antelope, then I know I've become a baby. No, don't give me to him! Frowning baby. Don't worry, it's all right. The touch of the water soothes me. The word "caress" appears, uninvited. I'm being caressed and unravelled by the movement of the water. Mountain smells on the breeze. Patty is weaving and turning me in the water like oblivious seaweed. Total immersion. She folds and stretches me out. And it goes on and on.

After a possibly very long time she sets me down the right way up, tenderly placing my feet on the bottom of the pool as she steadies me. I find my feet, and then my balance. As I adjust, my eyelids gradually begin to move apart and a funny thing happens. Patty is smiling, there right in front of me, her face close to my face. As my eyes slowly open, I involuntarily utter a little noise. Not a moan – I am British for God's sake – more of a croak: a small sound of gratitude and surprise. It just bursts out of my mouth. And I'm not even embarrassed.

She smiles again, says "Take your time," and swims away from me. I look around. I'm too stunned to take in anything beyond the sight of my arms and legs. They are covered in small silver bubbles that tickle my skin. I wipe them away: they fizz up to the surface, then immediately return, silvering my skin. I do this a few times, slowly and a bit stupidly, like someone under hypnosis. The water is fizzy. I didn't even know. I love it.

Somehow I get out of the water and find my way back into my clothes. I am smiling, rumpled and dazed. I have probably grown a pulsating rainbow aura, or at the very least some kind of halo. I stagger off in search of Jean and Will. They have also been Harbined: I find them splashing around, naked, in the heart-shaped spring water pool. "The sign says 'Swimwear Optional' but no one's wearing any," says Jean, "so we just joined in."

We may have resisted the *Vagina Monologues*, but apparently we're ripe for conversion here. I tell her about my small croak, and we have a fit of laughter. Will is getting sleepy, and we're in danger of becoming hysterical, so we settle him down in his buggy and go for a walk along a mountain path. The wooden sign says "Serenity Trail". As we go, we joke about my croak. What was it? The final gasp of the Dragon of the Crock? The renunciation of a life of hippy-resenting?

The Croak of Acceptance. On Serenity Trail. We laugh like drunken teenagers, and Will conks out in minutes.

In the quiet space of Will's sleep, Jean and I relax in the Blue Café. As well as bathing, massage and being reborn, Harbin offers courses in such things as 'Timeless Loving', 'Sky-Dancing Tantra' and 'Let the Crazy Child Write'. I observe this straight-faced; I've lost the capacity for sarcasm and I don't even care. Some people walk by wearing only bracelets and body art. We share a vegan black-bean burrito and pumpkin cake with our almond-milk lattes. For all my professed antipathy to anything patchouli-flavoured, I'm doing pretty well. The day floats ever so gently onwards.

At some point Jean drives us back home, slowly, through this land of languorous valleys and trees so massive that you can see the centuries. We agree that it'd be rude not to drink all that in. The Porter Creek vineyard in the Russian River Valley is a properly delicious place to stop off. Oh go on then, why not? Several locals are milling around, here to try the latest offerings.

The beardy owner looks as unlike a starchy sommelier as is humanly possible. I tell him about my Wollstonecraft trail, and he mentions that Robert Louis Stevenson travelled through California's nascent wine valleys, making free with the local goodness. Stevenson wrote:

In this wild spot, I did not feel the sacredness of ancient cultivation. It was still raw... yet the stirring sunlight and the growing vines and the vats and bottles in the cavern made a pleasant music for the mind. Here, also, earth's cream was being skimmed and garnered: and the customer can taste,

*such as it is, the tang of the earth in this green valley. So
local, so quintessential is a wine that it seems the very birds
in the veranda might communicate a flavour...*

I am drinking California. I've been rebirthed as a Harbin love
child and now I'm imbibing the birdsong and greenery, in glass
after glass of sunlit wine. Jean has gone off playing around in
the garden with Will – as today's driver, she's not indulging.
They leave me to get lightly, goldenly intoxicated by myself.
I become talkative and tremendously witty, engaging my co-
tasters in unsolicited anecdotes about Mary Wollstonecraft.
No one seems to mind. It's mellow. Mellow! Did I really just
say that?

Wine and life haven't tasted this good since that blinding
orchestral moment at the end of Norway's silver trail. We travel
the full grape spectrum, and I try out wines that are described
as "fruit-forward" and "earth-driven", immediately evoking
Annie Sprinkle. I roll them lasciviously around my mouth,
playing with them, allowing them to come into me. Annie
would be proud. Even the wine is ecosexual in California.

*The forest exhales a wild perfume, mixed with a thousand
nameless sweets that, soothing the heart, leave images in the
memory which the imagination will ever hold dear.*

Chapter Eighteen

*"Acquire Sufficient Fortitude to
Pursue Your Own Happiness"*

In the end, it's something very small that breaks unexpectedly into the Californian spell. There've been a few phone calls and emails from my beloveds back home, but not many. Then this morning an email arrives. Justin has sent a short recording of Eva's violin practice. The scratchy sound comes out of my phone, and it's like treading on a pin. I can hear Elsa and Zola chattering in the background. These small common sounds cut deep, it's the sound of home. It hurts, and I know immediately that we've been away for the right amount of time. Any longer will be too much.

Saying goodbye to Jean and Doug isn't easy, but I'm also elated. Not only by the trees, wine and food, but by the many answers I've gathered. "It's so much easier now," I tease Jean. "The next time we're asked about feminism, we can say: 'I'm identifying as a post-binary, non-gender ecosexual right now. I may well shift along the continuum this evening or next week.'"

Time is running out, the time of this trip. Will and I spend our last night in a hotel, and I'm transcribing my interviews furiously during his midday sleep. The remaining moments feel almost countable. The moments of this rainbow life on the road with my baby. They're finite. Just the thought of this makes me take the risk of going over, leaning into his cot and lightly touching his hair. His chest rises and falls gently.

Has this whole thing been an excuse to revel more deeply in the last baby days of my last baby? Repeating ripples of thought about how he's growing up become regular waves, waves of a tender sadness. With every new thing he learns, he is deeper into the world and further from me. The mysterious bud of Will blossoms more every day. His babyhood is now behind us.

I ache with a sudden longing for the lost moments. Something comes back from the past, lines that I learnt off by heart when I still didn't know what they meant. It's from a poem by Goethe, a contemporary of Wollstonecraft. He was writing about a woman, but it could just as well be Will scampering on that Californian beach with his hair stuck down in the wind and his belly poking out:

> *Ich besaß es doch einmal*
> *Was so köstlich ist*
> *Dass man doch zu seiner Qual*
> *Nimmer es vergisst!*

I possessed it once:
That which is so exquisite
That to my torment
I can never forget it!

Wollstonecraft too leant over her baby, on those far Scandinavian shores, blessed her sleeping face, heard her small feet pattering on the sand. She too felt the loss of the moment. You can only see it as it moves away. This is why, when you're holding your newborn, smitten women lurch up to behold it with their tear-stung eyes. You patiently repeat: "It's a girl… four weeks old… six and half a pounds." But they don't really care about all that. What they want is to reclaim their own baby in yours. They can't believe it, because they are seeing the thing that they have lost forever.

Soon Will and I will be all the way back into the torrent of the real world: shouting kids, falling out with friends, shoes everywhere, school rush, laundry, deadlines, childcare, work, getting everyone fed and then doing it all over again. This is our last precious bubble of exclusive time. Somehow it's heightened by Will's complete oblivion, as I gaze on his sleeping face.

But even screechy mornings trying to get everyone into their shoes and out the front door – even these are "moments". And this is why the squeaking violin causes such a stab in my heart. At home it'd be a background irritation. Here it is singled out, amplified with all the grandeur of a church organ and given meaning. That small sound is part of my life and all the meaning of my life.

My child was sleeping with equal calmness – innocent and sweet as the closing flowers. Some recollections … made a tear drop on the rosy cheek I had just kissed, and emotions that trembled on the brink of ecstasy and agony gave a poignancy to my sensations which made me feel more alive than usual.

Wollstonecraft stares at her baby and goes on to talk about being not an island, but part of the grand mass of humanity – just as I am feeling the magnetic pull of home. Those ancient domestic resentments have been ironed out by some newer freedoms. They are freedoms that were hard-won, and not by me. They are freedoms I didn't appreciate before, and they are tempered by knowing not everyone can do this. What about the Lago showgirls and the Holbeck estate mums. What about them?

Well, even if it's been a selfish journey, the witches taught me not to let that bring me down. We're picking up what's right in front of us. Above all, I'm dying to see Justin and the girls again. What led me away from home has now brought me closer. There's no place like it. And I've officially given up caring if I sound like I'm on the mommy drugs.

It lashes down with dark grey rain on our last day. It pours down the back of my neck as I load Will into his car seat this one last time, on our way back to San Francisco International Airport. Even Ms Satnav seems a bit sullen. We have to do a huge loop around Presidio because she kept silent. Funny how things get faster at the end, like the last few grains of sand speeding through the hourglass. I've packed in a blur. If I get searched I definitely hope they find my Annie Sprinkle DVD: *How To Be a Sex Goddess: Action Tips from Post-Modern Porn.*

But the writing – the impulse to record it all, the clapping of the net over the butterfly of the moment – was it useful? I have spent a thousand hunched hours on it. Hours spent away from my kids, but writing about them. Often without knowing why. I was on it, so I kept going. The usefulness or otherwise of this is debatable. What is beyond debate is the power of the book that made me do it. *Letters from Norway*, and the multi-directional adventures bursting from its yellowing pages. Her centuries-old words reinforced the need to go out and live things a bit deeper, right now. And then, that haunting call, to

form your grand principles of action, to save you from the vain regret of having, through irresolution, let the spring tide of existence pass away, unimproved, unenjoyed. Gain experience – ah, gain it! – while experience is worth having, and acquire sufficient fortitude to pursue your own happiness; it includes your utility, by a direct path…

Will and I set off with one set of Grand Principles of Action:

1) to make more people love Wollstonecraft
2) to follow her legacy forwards
3) to think about motherhood instead of just doing it

and managed to clock up some new ones quite by accident:

4) to quell the hippy rage
5) to want more than anything to come home

It didn't always seem like a direct path. But it did lead us directly out the front door, out of the daily scramble of hurrying and stuff and squabbling and laundry and whatever else it is that makes it suddenly be much later than you thought.

Because life spreads out like a spilt glass of water, running its way, in a small and brief trickle. For a short time, we took the water off its course and managed to freeze it, lift it up and look through it. And that was enough. Let that spilt water go, evaporate, form a cloud elsewhere; I can call it a day.

Surely something resides in this heart that is not perishable – and life is more than a dream?

Wollstonecraft stood alone and stands alone. I never wanted to be an expert, just a companion. And for her thoughts; her courage and indignation, to accompany others too. "I do not wish [women] to have power over men, but over themselves." What could be more powerful than completing a quest? Even if it was a quest that I couldn't properly see until we'd done it.

The very end of the trip too suddenly arrives, and we're on the flight home. Will only thrashes for almost an hour, and then he falls into the deepest, dearest sleep. I flop my head back on the seat. I'm tired, but it's not the grinding exhaustion of everyday motherhood: it's a profoundly satisfying tiredness. My mind has run up and down several mountains of thought, while my body carried this baby along for the ride. There's an elated sadness that doesn't stem entirely from this double gin-and-tonic. Cheers, Wolly. We did it. I sigh theatrically, disturbing the hair of the man sitting in front of us. I don't care. We've done the three journeys and now I can come home.

When I pulled Will out of his warm cot, all those long months ago, and set off on that bright early morning to Norway, I had no idea what we'd find. Or that what we would find might lead us onwards to further and bigger adventures. Together we flew against the scarcely perceptible current of daily life, the current that floats us along, ushering us beyond the moment and into old age without noticing; letting

the spring tide of existence pass away, unimproved, unenjoyed.

I expected to chase some freedoms and have some fun. I wasn't looking for searing insights into my own existence. And don't worry: I haven't found any, and am resolutely continuing not to look. So that's OK and you can cut the end theme music swell right there. But I'd be lying if I pretended that I've managed not to learn anything. On top of the stuff I actually wanted to learn, that is, about Wollstonecraft and women's lives. It turns out that it's not selfish to

acquire sufficient fortitude to pursue your own happiness.

There were surprises, too. So many other worlds are all happening at the same time – you can take your pick – but there's one thing they have in common. It's that people are basically better than you may expect. They are kinder, more willing to share and much funnier than I ever hoped. This is worth putting to the test some time. Even with a baby. Especially with a baby...

Gain experience – ah, gain it!

The answers are all flying around my head, clashing and spinning like glitter in a snow globe. What matters? What is it that matters? I look down at Will: he's dreaming in his traditional spot in the next seat. Legs resting on my legs, arms flung up over his head, eyelids soft. I pick up his left foot and hold it for almost the whole flight. It fits into my hand. This won't last. There's everything I've learnt and then there's this, right now, the best thing ever.

Acknowledgements

From the outset this book relied on the goodwill and generosity of others. I have an immense debt of gratitude to every person who appears in its pages, including those whose names have been changed to protect identities. If you're in here: I love, thank and owe you a big one, for ever.

Some of the travel was funded by the Society of Authors' K. Blundell Trust Award. The Society's work promoting the interests and the very existence of writers is increasingly important, and much appreciated (www.societyofauthors.org).

Special behind-the-scenes thanks to Mark Skipworth, and to my wonderful agent Adrian Sington.

Thanks to my SOWsters, Rachel, Tahmima and Kamila – truly: without whom, and all that.

Huge thanks to the formidable combo of Alessandro Gallenzi and Elisabetta Minervini, and to everyone at Alma Books. What a joy to be published by you.

Thank you Mary Wollstonecraft. Thank you Yorkshire Tea. Does anyone read this part? I'll just carry on… Thank you for buying this book. Please keep on buying books. Books are magic. Thank you, Books. Tha— what? OK, I'll stop.